MARTHA'S PEARLS

A SPIRITUAL APPROACH TO LIFE

MARTHA CREEK

CONTENTS

If you haven't yet had the privilege of experiencing the gift of Martha Creek, this book will provide you with wondrous insights to facilitate your journey to awakening. This profound, simple book needs to be read slowly and savored for higher understanding and remembrance. Martha totally lives and owns what she writes. Within these pages, you can feel the presence of her full hearted soul who is here to love you, to see your radiance, and to serve you. If you've heard Martha give a presentation, then you know that her love for you is palpable. Reading her words is like hearing her voice in person, telling you the stories of transformation and truth.

It is with deepest of gratitude to have had the privilege of working alongside Martha, sharing the ministry of Unity of Louisville since 2001 until my retirement in 2013. I witnessed her generosity, wisdom, service, joy, clarity, love, strength and peace. She brightens our world as she lives in joy every day. She inspires us to evolve spiritually, to see beyond our limits, and leads us to awaken to our divinity. Her numerous accomplishments reflect her compassionate heart and spirit.

Allow Martha to fill your heart and soul through her words. She invites you to live in the now moment, seeing and trusting what is possible. Be inspired to transform your life to being more than what you thought it could be. Remember your divinity, for your life is a grand adventure of joy!

-Rev. Susan EngPoole

INTRODUCTION

As I think about *Martha's Pearls* being brought to life, I am deeply humbled by the whole notion. I have been asked a thousand times, "When are you going to write a book?" Tired of hearing it, I mostly responded with, "Never! Never! Never!" So again, I was wrong. I can happily admit I don't mind being wrong and relish in the miracle of that.

I have been writing for as long as I could hold a pen. I won every spelling bee in my fourth grade class but one (that's another book), and consistently stand amazed at what words can do for the human spirit, to light our way, to enlighten our minds, to enliven our being, to inspire, to teach, to heal, to forgive, to make regrets, to make amends, and to remember who and whose we are.

So, I offer these humble snippets of loving, learning, and being with a wholehearted prayer that you are served in miraculous ways.

In spirit and love, Martha

TESTIMONIALS

"*Next to God, Martha Creek may be the wisest, most wonderful teacher on the planet. I turn cartwheels in gratitude that our paths crossed. Thank you, Martha, for well, everything!!!*" —Pam Grout, #1 New York Times bestselling author of 19 books

"*There are few people in my life, that when I meet them, I have an instant recognition of authenticity, depth of knowing and pure love. I call these people 'the real deal.' Martha is the real deal. If you have the opportunity to be in her orbit, I heartfully encourage you to give yourself the gift of Martha. Big love.*" —Rev. Jude Denning, Senior Minister, Unity of Stuart, FL

"*Martha Creek is an enlightened being and passionate speaker who engages and facilitates an honest realization of who we truly are. Profoundly real and liberating, Martha walks her talk and challenges each of us to do the same.*" —Rev. Greg Coles, M.Div.

"Martha's down home, bottom line, 'what is, is' way of being is a teacher to us all. Martha doesn't just own the knowledge, she is the knowledge!" —Janet Bray Attwood, Co-Author of New York Times Bestseller, *The Passion Test*

"Martha is a powerful presence for quality and professionalism. She serves being audaciously sincere and forthright and she provides confidence, competence, and clarity!" —Rev. John McLean, Senior Minister - Unity of Nashville

"Martha is a dynamic, authentic being, living out her best, current understanding of who she is. She serves by being open and available to everyone and provides an environment of exploration, encouraging honest and courageous participation. Love you!" —Rev. Vicki Vanderhorst, Unity Minister Canada

"Martha is a well-known teacher, trainer and facilitator. She serves by modeling authenticity. Her works provides basic truths that are beneficial not only in your spiritual community's leadership, but also in your personal life. I am a better minister, spiritual leader, partner, mother, daughter and friend because of my connection to Martha Creek and her teachings." —Denise Yeargin, Retired Unity Minister

"Martha's embracing yet confronting spirit has brought deep inner growth and a greater bond of mutual respect and love for our organization and teams." —Rev. Chris Jackson, Senior Minister, Unity on the Bay - Miami, FL

"Martha has the invaluable gift of telling even hard truths with love and compassion. Her teaching, counsel and work help those she works with discover new depths of courage and wisdom. She's able to provide comfort and courage to those who need uplifting; and she'll deliver a highly effective kick in the consciousness to those who need motivating." —Rev. Kurt Condra, Senior Minister, Unity on the North Shore

"Rev. Martha Creek has created a beautiful mark on my being. She has taught me how to focus my thoughts, to simplify and yet evaluate with depth and honest appraisal the inner messages being sent my way. She encourages love in all forms and the exploration of a well lived life, facing every fear, turning every corner, and by all means, celebrating every moment." —Noell Rowan, PhD, Wilmington, NC

"Martha has the innate ability to hold your heart and sometimes your hand as she leads you back to yourself- your own wisdom, your own integrity." —Diane Czerwonka, A life forever changed.

1

ISSUMAGIJOUJUNGNAINERMIK

In his book, *Facing Your Giants,* Max Lucado tells a story about Moravian missionaries struggling to find a word in the Inuit native language for the word forgiveness. They finally settled on *Issumagijoujungnainemik,* an assembly of letters that is literally translated as, *"not able to think about it anymore."*

Wouldn't it be wonderful to literally be "not able to think about it anymore?" What is it in your life or who is it that you have not forgiven? What is the giant in your life? What would facing it look like? What aspect of EGO keeps you stuck in it?

One day, Momma was talking about not liking a woman and I asked her the basis for her dislike. She said because the woman lied about her one time. That could seem like grounds for unforgiveness. Right? Trusting that people are going to do what people do seems more forgiving to me. It's a saner alternative than believing that they are going to do what I want them to do. Well, what if you knew this happened when Momma was five years old and that it was about a coloring book being colored in? Yes, a lifetime of not liking someone because...

In the spirit of being honest, I admit that in the past I often denied when I was holding something against somebody. I confess that I was bound by petty things from the past, like getting a "B" in high school. Yes, one "B" and I blamed the teacher for it. Then, there was a random man on a beach one time 30 years ago that made some crack about my weight. (Never mind that I thought the same thing.) And, my brother threw a deck of cards at me and caused a black eye the week of eighth grade graduation and I was Valedictorian. I could go on for a hundred years about all the "small" unforgivenesses I carried in an attempt to elevate myself above the BIG ones.

With all the many books, workshops, theories, lectures, processes, and practices on forgiveness, it still doesn't necessarily make the task of carrying it out as easy as it may seem, or that we might prefer. Is it actually even possible to forgive?

God knows we can hold the intention of forgiving someone for whatever it is that we think they did to us. Sometimes we believe we have worked through a relationship or situation and can check that one off the box until something brings it back to us with a little thread hanging for us to grab hold of and pull. When that button is pushed or the memory or familiar feeling is evoked, we are hostage to the hurt.

Author and friend the late Colin Tipping (www.

colintipping.com) notes in his book *Radical Forgiveness* that being able to forgive others is one thing, but forgiving ourselves is a lot harder. He also talked about the difference between making a decision to give up resentment and actually doing it. His technique and practices include worksheets, letter writing, reframing situations, and guidance for our willingness to entertain the possibility of spiritual perfection in every situation.

Look at the word itself — forgive (for-give). As in, we are giving ourselves freedom and letting ourselves off the hook as we offer forgiveness to others. It is in giving that we receive. Does that sound familiar?

I am grateful for my father, Joe, who truly lived out forgiveness. He seemed immune to the chronic nature of ill will, harboring, regretting, blaming, etc. I asked him many, many questions during his final years and his replies were short and clear.

"It doesn't do any good to hold things against people.
I've learned about people by what they do."

This never seemed like forgiveness to me, simply wisdom to trust people to do what they do, not what I want them to do.

"I don't regret the past, I can't change it and I'm not going to live the rest of what life I have, imprisoned by it. I would do it differently IF I could, and I can't."
—Joe H. Creek, 1933–2007

I believe that to truly know God, we must learn to understand the weaknesses and imperfections of others. How can we do that unless we understand our own? How can we see our own limitations until we become aware of God's mercy?

Forgiveness and compassion begin with forgiving ourselves—or with *Issumagijoujungnainermik*—(not able to think about it anymore).

2

IT'S MY LIFE, I'LL CRY IF I WANT TO

I've witnessed, time and again, the healing power of tears. Tears are our body's release valve for stress, sadness, grief, anxiety, and frustration. Also, we can have tears of joy, say when a child is born or we've been deeply touched; or tears of relief when a difficulty or fear has passed. In my own life, I am grateful when I can cry and I seldom ever hold back tears. I've been criticized as a public speaker for shedding tears and I've been acclaimed for shedding tears while speaking. It represents the full polarity of the judgments we hold about crying.

Crying feels cleansing, a way to purge pent-up emotions so they don't lodge in our bodies as stress symptoms such as fatigue or pain. It also feels authentic and natural to express this part of our humanity. To stay healthier, care for ourselves and release stress, I encourage us all to cry. WHY NOT?

Our bodies produce three kinds of tears: reflex,

continuous, and emotional. Each kind has different healing roles. For instance, reflex tears allow our eyes to clear out noxious particles when they're irritated by smoke or exhaust. The second kind, continuous tears, are produced regularly to keep our eyes lubricated, which functions as an anti-bacterial and protects our eyes from infection. Typically after crying, our breathing and heart rate decrease, and we enter into a calmer biological and emotional state.

Emotional tears have special health benefits. Biochemist and tear expert, Dr. William Frey, at the Ramsey Medical Center in Minneapolis, discovered that reflex tears are 98% water, whereas emotional tears also contain stress hormones that get excreted from the body through crying. After studying the composition of tears, Dr. Frey found that emotional tears shed these hormones and other toxins that accumulate during stress. Additional studies also suggest that crying stimulates the production of endorphins, our body's natural pain killer and feel-good hormones.

Crying makes us feel better, even when a problem persists. In addition to physical detoxification, emotional tears heal the heart. Don't hold tears back. Clients and friends sometime say, "Please excuse me for crying. I'm sorry I am crying. I was trying hard not to. It makes me feel weak." These and other similar sentiments often come from parents who were uncomfortable around tears, bearing shame and guilt for crying. They reflect a societal message that tells us we're weak for crying and for the perceived risk of being seen as weak.

My heart goes out to people when I hear this. I encourage them to keep their throat open and allow the tears. I invite them to be friendlier to tears, to welcome them in fact. The new enlightened paradigm of what constitutes a powerful man and woman is someone who has the strength and self-awareness to cry. These are the people who impress me, who I can trust to be honest in expression and wise enough to reap the benefits of a natural relief to stress.

A study performed at the University of Florida found that crying is more effective than any antidepressant on the market. A good cry improved the mood of 88.8% of weepers with only 8.4% reporting that crying made them feel worse.

Try to let go of outmoded, untrue, conceptions about crying. It is good to cry. It is healthy to cry. It helps to emotionally clear sadness and stress. Crying is also essential to resolve grief when waves of tears periodically come over us after we experience a loss. Tears help us process the loss so we can keep living with open hearts. Otherwise, we are set up for depression if we suppress these potent feelings.

There is an old Jewish proverb that says, *"What soap is for the body, tears are for the soul."*

Crying is a prescription. Take as needed and enjoy the relief, less pain, less stress, and heart-healing.

3

LIGHTEN UP

"When in doubt, lighten up."
—Martha Creek

February is my birthday month, therefore I tend to spend it celebrating, cruising, traveling and purposefully having expressive, creative fun, to remind me of the value and importance of "lightening up."

Being the oldest, responsible and serious child, it is not naturally easy for me to play, frolic and lighten up. I don't actually really work at having fun, I just have to be more deliberate to ensure that all work and no play does not keep me stuck in the patterned way of functioning that seems to rule sometimes.

For many years, I have traveled with a big yellow foam wig affectionately referred to as the "bigwig." I actually have several of them that others in the travel group adorn along with me to bring an ambush of joy, play and playfulness to many interesting situations. For example, on a cruise, people from all over the world run up to us and want to take a photo, or to try the wig on, or to get their friends and family involved.

The staff of the cruise seems extremely grateful for the lighter side of their intentionally fun guests, and often become part of our antics and celebration as well. A few years ago, the dinner staff, maître'd, head waiters, table servers, etc., even the cruise director and captain, were enjoying our outrageous inclusive, extravagant, purposeful fun and joined in on a daily and nightly basis. The dining room staff would peek out from their assigned stations and line up; waiting for us to arrive to see what prelude of joy was in store. The "bigwig" clan actually received a shout-out from the cruise director. A real first!

At the annual Creek clan cookout and fall celebration, the elders in our community get a chance to lighten up, wear funny hats and glasses and be kids again. They are so excited at the opportunity for these antics and they don't have to be encouraged to wear the silly things. They are often in line for their turn. It makes my heart sing to see proof that wisdom definitely comes with age.

To my surprise, more and more of the elders have asked me to send them an email, post it on Facebook, or get them a copy to show their family and co-workers. They are naturally and socially paying the joy forward. Enlightened beings need no encouragement for fun and play. What a graceful reminder for me to keep it light and lighter.

4

MOTHER! WHERE ARE YOU?

I f you were stranded on a desert island and could have only one book with you, what would it be? For many years, my answer was Marianne Williamson's *A Return to Love*. In this bestseller, she states that our mother creates our first image/impression of an adult woman in our lives. Our experience of Mother is one that can influence our experience of women throughout our lives.

My dear friends gifted me with a ticket to see the Judd's at Louisville's new Yum Center in December 2011. I have enjoyed the Judd's music and story since they first hit the country music scene decades ago. In one of their interviews, I was struck by their transparency as the Judd's talked about their story of Mother Naomi and teenage daughter Wynonna growing up living together on a tour bus. Imagine being this close to your mother day-in-and-day-out in this unusual living arrangement, not to mention the pressures of careers. Yikes! Except for the stardom, I believe their story is also basically our story; one that includes conflict and heartache and is also full of understanding, mutual respect, survival, growth, self-realization, fun times and love.

We carry so many loaded stories of how our mothers hurt us, did or didn't do something for us, how they said or didn't say what we wanted, and so on. Now, for our sake, let's ask ourselves: Who would I be without my story of mother? I would be more compassionate and understanding of her life and her journey to motherhood; amazed at how she managed through challenges; awake to how well she did in the big scheme of things; meeting her as a friend instead of with a "should" club. I would be more curious about the woman who raised me; more grateful for what I have and had instead of what I should have had; more amused at the drama that I've watched like an old rerun for most of my life; and for sure, more present to my own life and the bounty of blessings obvious to anyone.

If you are a mother, who would you be and how would you treat yourself and your children differently if you didn't think and believe that you had to uphold or live out your unquestioned, false story of "Mother" and all that should be? How would your life and theirs be better off, without believing these old ancient concepts?

One of the most powerful exercises for me during my work with the Hoffman Institute—week-long process that provides a safe, supportive environment in which participants identify and begin healing negative patterns of feeling, thinking, and behaving in any kind of relationship— was having an imagined conversation with each parent asking them about their childhood experiences, difficulties, sorrows, joys and successes. I also wrote twelve full pages to both parents stating all that I wanted to speak/say that I had not. For the last part of the exercise, I wrote back as though my parents were writing to me. The gift of this experience was the revelation of just how much I loved them and how deeply I truly wanted to free them from all the ick that I had naively put on them as shoulds, wants, needs and false beliefs. As I took them off the hook, guess who got free?

Be the mother you may have always wanted for you. It isn't necessary to give birth to have the experience of mothering. Find ways that you can mother you and those around you in your life. You may be the only experience of Mother that a person has ever had.

5

NEVER, NEVER GIVE UP

What is the scope and the landscape of the day-to-day/week-to-week events in your life? Does it seem bountiful or bleak? During any given week, mine might include planning a slumber party for a friend in hospice care, celebrating loved ones birthdays, welcoming a dear friend's granddaughter into the world, planning for an upcoming retirement, meeting a host of new friends and reaching out, holding space in prayer for those affected by an earthquake or hurricane. I notice that less and less I call things good or bad or right or wrong. Truly realizing it is all divinely appointed and part of my soul's evolution (whether I like it or not) enables me to oppose "what is" much less often and allows me to give my energy and attention to how I can serve and support.

In coping with and navigating life's challenges, I have a practice of questioning stressful thoughts. This is a radical turnaround to the typical way of experiencing life. I approach the stressful thoughts from a perspective of: "How am I better off in this?" Such as: How am I better off that my brother died? How am I better off that I had breast cancer? How am I better off that my flight home was canceled? Are you aware of the resistance you have from just reading this? Could challenges actually reveal something good?

Just questioning instead of reacting fearfully can create enough space between me and the thinking that it allows for a light to shine in on the apparent darkness, sadness, loneliness, resentment, or such. I can actually begin to find and appreciate the blessings of what is, what I have, what I had, and actually see some ways that I am better off for it. One thing I know for sure is that reality is kinder than my stressful opposing thoughts.

I had a friend, Sister Mary Rhodes, (Rhodie) who lived in the Motherhouse at Loretto, Kentucky. When Rhodie retired at about age 86, she told me she was moving to the Motherhouse so she could serve the residents in the infirmary there. I met Rhodie when I first moved to Louisville, Kentucky and she and I lived in the same apartment building. I was awed and inspired by her from the first time we met. Rhodie was fearless. She told me once she had been hit by a car while crossing the slippery winter street. I reminded her that I could drive her to her job and duties, particularly in the dark, winter months. Rhodie seemed as shocked as if I had put a stun gun on her. She quickly and clearly replied, "I am only 83, I can walk." She had more awards for volunteer service than I have ever seen and I have no idea the full extent of her service. I know it included more than 50 years of teaching and thousands of hours volunteering. In addition to being fearless, Rhodie was brilliant, funny, expressive, inquisitive, generous, spunky and a shining example of stewardship. She experienced several broken bones, health challenges and various problems during her retirement and therefore lived in the infirmary instead of "in service."

During her late nineties, Rhodie experienced Alzheimer's but was still a "way-shower" for living. On one visit with her, Rhodie asked me who I was. She did so with such strength and courage. I was profoundly struck by how the disease could not take her essence. After I told her who I was and how we met, she quickly went into telling my favorite story about her mother, the post mistress of Loretto. During our visit, I gave her a gift plaque for her room that said, "Never, Never Give Up." Her eyes lit up like crystals, her smile aglow and in her exuberant spirit, she began repeating the statement out loud with glee and joy, "Never, Never Give Up." "Never, Never Give Up." She then, naturally, began to pass it around for the other residents to enjoy and share. That was her way of gifting everybody.

Reality: The gift was obviously for me as I watched her eyes come to life and her essence radiate in joy. There was no disease or dis-ease in that moment. Instead, it was perfect.

What is going on in your life that could easily cause you to give up on your dreams, loved ones, friends, careers, the economy, health, or world peace? Who would you be in exactly the same situation not calling it a problem or making it wrong? What if you simply do what you can do?

Never, never give up on the possibility that God is Good and FOR SURE—so are you.

6

PERSPECTIVE OR TRUTH?

What does the change in seasons bring for you or mean to you? I notice that with all the travelling I do that it doesn't really register too much with me anymore. One day, I am in the tip of Maine, then off to Florida. The next week it could be Bugtussle, Kentucky or Belfast, Ireland.

In 2015, I traveled to Ireland with one of the most joyous and fun groups of people I've ever been on a trip with. We had tremendously wonderful tour guides native to Ireland; a well-balanced schedule; and the miracle of all miracles of weather in Ireland. I was there nine days and it didn't rain once. Even the locals were talking about what a miracle this was.

Sometimes we forget that life is really a series of miracles. As I listened to the ongoing history, stories, and tales of Ireland, I became more and more aware of how our perspectives vary, get muddled, cloudy, are too rigid, and can often be mistaken for the truth. While I do not claim to know any truth, I am more and more aware of the tendency to believe I do. It is alarming the hold the mind can have on me/us even when we are intent on loosening and questioning it.

By the time I visit Ireland again, I will have traveled to other countries and parts of the United States. It's a good thing I can keep my perspectives loose and my heart open to variances in the way we are, the way we do things, the way we think, and the ways of the world. Can you imagine all the ways I see a bed made, the toilet paper over and under, the seat up, the seat down, the dishes faced out, the dishes faced in, the towels double and triple folded, the lights on, the lights off, the door left open, the door left closed, the pets in, the pets out and everything in between in our beautiful and challenging humanity? They ALL reflect aspects of mySELF and I feel blessed and better for it.

Whether you are traveling the world or simply traveling through life, remember to choose what matters to you. If you see something you don't like, choose again, gain perspective, see it differently or simply make a wish.

7

PRACTICE MAKES PROGRESS

I have had the privilege and practice of celebrating my birthday for more than 60 years! As a work in progress, I am willing, and did, enjoy every song, every call, every text, every prayer, every blessing, every posting, every card and every wish as it has evolved.

In reflection, I am reminded of the lyrics from my friend, singer, and songwriter David Roth's song, "Practice Makes Progress." David and I shared an event in Melbourne, Florida. Those attending were blessed with first-hand experience of David's heartfelt messages in song. It's great fun to be with David and especially when he says, "Practice makes _____," and the audience exuberantly responds with "Perfect." He quickly and slyly comes in with the word "Progress." His response is more reality based. Practice makes progress, not perfection.

Some of the ways I have observed progress from my practices in my human journey include:

- Taking sensible action toward solving crisis, problems, and possibilities—with less attachment.
- Less and less jumping in to please.
- Building my tolerance with discomfort in others —accepting that discomfort, stress, pain, and suffering are all vital parts of the human learning process and understanding the value of it. NO suffering is in vain.
- Staying quiet and allowing other members of the group to respond instead of being the first to respond when a question goes out to the group.
- Accepting standing alone sometimes.
- Allowing time for things to process.
- More patience with self and others.
- Questioning concepts and false meanings.
- Taking down the old archaic framework of wrong and right, and replacing it with a lens of what is—is.

It all sounds easy, right? Try it on!

Over one of my actual birthday weekends, I had the opportunity to experience allowing a book to be written through me. This idea poured through me, literally, for approximately 30 hours during three days of spirit-led writing. Although writing a book was a new experience for me, there wasn't much doubt in me that I could do it. I just didn't have a prior experience of doing it. It's a very different thing to have an experience of what you think something will be like, versus actually doing it. I now have an experience of the writing doing me.

This may be similar to how athletes say they are able to finish a marathon or some challenge they didn't think they could, but because they were in the flow, they did. For me, it was an experience of the writing actually doing me and losing all track and reference to time.

What are you practicing and where is your progress? Make sure to acknowledge you and really get a sense of it. Practice makes—Progress! GIVE IT A TRY.

It's no little thing. You being you and me being me is a gift to our world.

8

RAISE THE PRAISE

In January 2017, I was strongly guided to *"raise the praise."* This really surprised me since I am honestly pretty mindful about giving and receiving praise. Truthfully, no matter how much I already do this, am this and believe this, there is always room for increase. The Universe rushes and continues to bring forth opportunities for me to have a rampage of praise.

It seems to me that getting back to basics is not only practical and purposeful but a heck of a lot easier than keeping the victimhood persona and ego running the show. This normal way of being is very draining, and, exhausting to me and, as I've observed first-hand, does not create much beyond what I already have.

January is a standard time to quit or let go of some things. It is a time when most of us launch into a new way of being. After my decision to up my praise game, I focused on one important quit each month. As I raised the praise and quit the energy leaks and drains, it seemed to have an exponential effect on my manifestations, creating life experiences that were more expansive and interesting.

I began with an "easy" quit: Being Afraid of What Others Think.

Sound easy? I can tell you that even after many years of practice, I am still not immune from this patterned way of being. Even though, and gratefully so, it is much slighter and rarer, I still notice and catch myself making decisions, plans, and responses based on what someone will think and/or believe about me instead of what is simply honest action for me.

For example: I took my car in to get routine service, prepared for the "up-sale" of the 30,000-mile package they offer. I stated, "I only want an oil change, fluid and filter check, standard routine maintenance." He responded with, "You are due for the 30,000-mile checkup." I said, "That is right (try saying someone is right and see what it stirs up in you) and I don't want that. I just want a standard routine maintenance."

An eternity in about 30 seconds transpired that included all the "whys" I need to do the 30,000 mile checkup. After asking just how much it would save me, compared to doing all the items separately and him assuring me of the great deal, discounting the original offer another $30, I agreed to it. The point here is not the value for the services or the money, but what I was aware of throughout the entire interaction—a very strong impulse to "go along," "get along," "be nice," "be agreeable," "don't make anybody mad," "convince him I'm nice," etc., etc., etc.

I realized I had much work to do. Instead of old behavior and thinking, I needed to anchor my wholeness in the love of God/Creator. I had to quit relying on the approval and acknowledgment of others for my sense of self-worth. I had to quit being afraid of thoughts from others, or from the crazy mind that recycles them since the beginning of time.

I have learned that if we quit some worry, and raise our practice of praise, we're sure to start some *new ways* of being that promises to *raise* our vibration and our possibilities. I have reignited some of my spiritual practices, including deepening my state of inquiry, *The Work, www.thework.com.* I am re-listening to *A New Earth* by Eckhart Tolle and have other spiritual teachers in queue for time together on purpose.

I invite you to remember what and who has helped you to live in integral ways and to reunite with that wise aspect of your*self*. Brush off that favorite book or CD series and play it again Sam.

9

(DIS) HONESTY

As a kid, the harshest words I heard coming from adults around me were "liar" and "lazy" as they criticized and labeled others. I didn't know what those words meant as a kid, I just knew they were bad and I must never be that or do that. Imagine for a moment the impact of this particular belief on a life.

As I've matured, (slightly—it's a process not perfection and certainly not a quick fix or destination) I can better accept the reality that it is normal human phenomena to lie and to be lazy. There is a time for all things—the alpha and omega. I understand the mind is filled with fear and torment from self judging notions that trigger survival. I'm aware that the mind gets so undone that it feels like it's a matter of life or death, even when there is no real threat.

When I reflect on what is happening within me when I lie, it's easier to have compassion for myself. I am normally afraid of offending someone or maybe hurting their feelings.

I don't want to leave them out or disconnect from them emotionally. I often want to maintain an identity, a persona, a reputation or position. For example, the desire to be seen as the generous one, or the flexible one, or the servant leader or the one people can count on, etc. The price is very high indeed. I am aware that I sometimes won't speak up to keep peace or to avoid argument and conflict. That is dis-honest for me at times, and I regret it afterwards.

The following are guidelines I use in examining my level of honesty:

- Leaving out pertinent information is no different than lying and is considered manipulative and dishonest.
- True integrity is when what we think, what we do, and what we say are in alignment.
- True honesty is when we can look at our own thoughts, words, and actions and admit we have some work to do, without projecting our guilt onto others (making them wrong). Jesus said it so well when he said, "Take the log out of your own eye before you take the speck out of your neighbor's eye."
- Paramount is being up front about how you think and feel, even though it may seem self-revealing, feels vulnerable, or may even be unacceptable to others.
- Liar. So? I continue a journey to honesty, accepting my own humanity and therefore realizing more compassion with yours.

People shouldn't lie = Fantasy.
People lie = Reality.
People should be honest = Fantasy.
People can be dishonest = Reality.
Reality is solid ground.

Take honesty and (dis) honesty to a new level and watch your life shift to a more enjoyable and honorable place! Help to bring heaven to earth—grounded in reality!

10

AMENDS

Compensation, Reparation, Indemnity, Recompense

A few years ago, during one of my visits with Momma, we were watching game shows. I was struck by one of the findings from the "American Bible Challenge Show." The question asked to poll 100 women was this: "Who is to blame from the Garden of Eden scene—Adam, Eve, or the Snake?" One hundred women were answering the question, "Who's to blame?"

Of the three contestant teams on the show, two were women and one was men. Both of the women's teams guessed that the polled women responded with "snake." The men's team guessed that the polled women responded with "men." What does this reveal about our thinking? What would be your answer?

However, the actual answer given by the polled women was "women." This means women think women are to blame for the core of human suffering. Another similar poll revealed men thought men were to blame. Neither in the polled group picked snake or the opposite gender. Are you scratching your head yet? This reveals our *Core Belief*: Regardless of gender, we *each think we are the cause of it, the fault of it, and the blame for it.*

This is the basis for my belief that ultimately our amends are to ourselves. It seems to make sense that all the angst, shame, blame, and guilt we experience is in fact caused when we "leave ourselves"—leave our true nature. Suffering ensues, such intense suffering that we displace it onto others to somehow attempt to relieve it from ourselves. If so, then shame, blame, and guilt all add great value to my life to show me where I am out of integrity with myself.

In the meantime, I am pursuing a thorough inquiry and trip through the past exploring interactions, thinking, actions, causes, effects, affects, consequences, and possibilities of what looking, seeing, telling the truth can do in amending, making right and setting me, we, the world free!

I was inspired earlier during this time to review the fourth step of the 12-Step sobriety process relative to amends/forgiveness/resentments, etc. a minister friend had written and facilitated writing several great articles about making amends in support of his church, Fellowship for Today. The following are snippets from his thoughts about surrender, sharing, restitution and guidance.

To surrender means essentially that we are to stop trying to be the director of the universe and we must give our lives back to where they truly are – with God. "Thy will, not mine, be done."

Sharing is finding out what is working and what is not working in our lives. Sharing requires that we take a personal inventory of our lives and share our findings with another person, such as a trusted friend, minister or sponsor.

Restitution is about determining which amends can be made directly to the person without harming anyone, and then doing so. We make all other amends indirectly.

Guidance means realizing that it is not about me, but rather what is good for all. Through prayer and meditation we receive the voice of God directing our affairs.

Who needs to make amends? I do! How about you?

What is amend-making? Here's how *wikihow.com* describes the process:

"Making amends is about trying to repair or compensate for something you did wrong that harmed another person in some way, causing them to feel insulted, or to suffer a loss, injury, or some sort of damage. When you are in the wrong, clinging to misguided notions of a need to "preserve your reputation" at all costs, or simply being stubborn, are poor options when a relationship is at stake and the ball rests in your court to do something about it. While it is never pleasant to feel ashamed about your own poor behavior, shame does have a place in life if it makes you acknowledge your wrongdoing and seek to make amends for it. And if you're in the situation of needing to make amends, there's no place like getting started." http://www.wikihow.com/Make-Amends

---

Our willingness and readiness is the key to effectiveness. Begin with a statement of regret of how your actions caused the other person harm, even though not intentionally. (You don't say the last phrase. Just the regret part is expressed to others.)

Accept responsibility for your actions. This means not blaming anyone else (including Adam, Eve or the snake) and not making excuses for what you did. Therefore, a statement of responsibility is needed.

Make clear your willingness to remedy the situation if it is called for. While you can't repair the past, you can repair the harm you caused. Give a meaningful offer of restitution or promise to take action so that you will not repeat the behavior(s).

It is helpful to review an amends letter with a trusted friend, therapist, minister, or sponsor. Keep your apology/amends completely one-sided. That means do not push for acceptance of your apology.

If you are ready, the following are a few more suggested pointers and questions to get you started. The Fourth Step is not meant to be an in-depth psychoanalysis of ourselves; rather it is asking God to awaken us to seeing where our lives have been out of alignment. It's really that simple! So say a short prayer asking to be shown what you need to see; then get on with your writing.

HONESTY:

(Is it true or is it false?)

How have I been dishonest with others and with myself?

Where have I lied, manipulated, cheated and stolen from others? List the big ones.

Who was hurt by my dishonesty?

How did this hurt my relationship with God, remembering that God is Truth? (If you don't believe in God, simply drop the word and use Truth for reference.)

UNSELFISHNESS:

(How will it affect others?)

How has self-centeredness shown itself in my life and who has been hurt by it?

Are there people, institutions or principles that still anger me? If so, what role have I played—either bringing it about or holding on to my resentment?

How have I put my own self-interest ahead of God's plan for me to be of service to others?

PURITY:

(Is it right or is it wrong?)

What past or present behaviors, thoughts or feelings make me feel guilty, isolated, or ashamed?

What are the areas of my life that I don't want others to see?

. . .

Remembering that my sex powers are God-given and good, where has my sex life strayed from what I believe is right?

LOVE:

(Is it ugly or is it beautiful?)

How has fear dominated my life?

Has my life been isolated—a lonely life of taking rather than giving?

Now, with God's help, am I ready to make love and service my code?

Who benefits from making amends? Me. You. Families. Communities. Races. Genders. Institutions. Health. The world!

Removing blocks: aligning to divine nature, daring to look; to say sorry; reconnecting to self and God; daring to ask for support, forgiveness and clarity; listening for guidance and refusing to hold anything against myself; I awaken again to a new, peaceful, and far more interesting life. I find multitudes of ways to love and serve myself, you and God. This is a beginning of amazing grace embodied and demonstrated.

11

AS WE GATHER WE CHANGE THE WORLD

Throughout our lifetime, many of us will gather together with family and friends for various reasons – holiday celebrations, birthdays, weddings, and funerals. For some it will be a time of religious celebrations and traditions. For others, it may be full of fun family traditions and travels. While for others, family gatherings, especially during the holiday season, can be less than magical. They can be stress-filled, anxiety-ridden, and touched with sadness or loneliness. Over the years, I've learned to expect and accept Both/And. The fantasy of the gatherings hasn't served me well and yet, I don't want the cynical aspect of mind that tantrums anytime something less than jolly enters the experience to rule the roost either.

I much prefer the thoughts of filling my time with family with thanks-living, joy and harmony. So, I live out and into the reality of Both/And. Instead of the old filing system of good/bad, I prefer to see and accept reality. Gathering with friends at dinners, parties and events = Good. Yes, of course, there are likely going to be some bristles in there too. Gathering with family/friends that we may not prefer, may not have much in common with or may not enjoy = Bad. Yes, in some ways it can be a bummer. In other ways, it can be simple feedback to me about where I am not honestly giving yes and no responses to requests. Missing family/friends who are no longer living and won't have a seat at the table = Bad. Not anymore.

If I live by the thought that I create my reality, then this is an opportunity to experience life from the Both/And. I may enjoy 99% of it and the 1% that I don't prefer may come right in and overshadow even the biggest joys. My biggest growth is to accept that I might as well welcome it all, minus the good and bad labels. The feelings of joy, happiness, reunion, connection, belonging, excitement of looking forward to—I welcome. The feelings of sadness, missing someone, feeling left out, feeling less than, lacking time, money, energy are also welcome. They are all such powerful, valuable teachers for us when we are open to the gift within each one.

This Both/And concept may be radical for some. It was for me when I first began self-inquiry and looking at my long-held beliefs, and even multi-generational patterns. All I can say is, if you are not experiencing the holidays or other family gatherings of your dreams, are not feeling the love, or are not looking forward to what is, you have options.

Without denying the loss, change, death, illness, and challenges in the world, we can also experience the rich, sweet, joy and bounty of this wonderful life.

If we have the courage to break out of patterns and thinking that no longer serve us or the world of change, or the courage to let our brilliant lights shine, we will know peace. We will know the kind of peace that is unshakably, undeniably based in presence and truth. We will know love so big that we can freely share it with others and embody it for ourselves.

12

BLOOM WHERE YOU'RE PLANTED

Brave, courageous, willing to stick their neck out, fearless to what's going on around them, opening up in all stages of grandeur—some a little bit at a time, some very quickly, and some remaining perfectly, tightly closed; this describes both the beautiful spring flowers that pop up in flower beds during the spring season and the precious souls I often witness in facilitation, sessions and workshops as they discover their beautiful selves while questioning stressful thoughts and recreating their stories.

Once at a *Loving What Is* workshop, I was given a vase of the most magnificent yellow daffodils. These blooms greeted me like a kiss from the warm sun. The daffodils became as much a part of the experience and curriculum as any worksheet handouts or exercises that weekend. I gave each participant a flower with the direction to let the flower speak to them and to learn from the flower. Each morning, the remaining flowers were more open and alive than the day before, and each night, each participant received another one. It was as though the flowers were opening and multiplying, literally serving as our transformation midwives. The participants' responses were sweet and meaningful. One after the other considered their similarity to the blossom and a new life being realized, thought-by-thought. Their inner reflections brought images of beauty, simplicity, tenderness, strength, vibrancy, vulnerability, courage, peace and openness. I love that flowers can be such powerful teachers for us.

After the workshop concluded, I received a letter of gratitude from a young woman. She shared how on her drive home, her thoughts had said, "Okay, now back to the real world. None of what I heard or experienced this past weekend will hold water in my real life." Her life, however, showed her those thoughts were not true because her life was different than it was before the workshop. When she returned to work on Monday morning, there was a new potted daffodil plant on her desk waiting to greet her. She realized that the work she had begun over the weekend would never end for her. She shared that for the first time in her life, she could see the parts of her that were immature, or not yet in bloom, without dark judgment but with a certain level of acceptance.

I have read and listened to Eckhart Tolle's *A New Earth* numerous times. It goes hand-in-hand with Byron Katie's *Loving What Is*. I have learned to always ask: What is true? This exercise can allow us to get in touch with the truth of who we are – our own divinity. It can be a sweet place for us to begin as we recognize our innate perfection, beauty, strength, and innocence—and, we do not have *to do* anything for it. Like the flowers, we are not the source or *the doing*. We are the expression; Presence itself. We cannot become *good* by working to be good or by doing good. We are good already and our opportunity is to find that reality inside ourselves. What a relief!!!!!! Now *that* is a breath of fresh spring air.

I invite you to the gift of *you* through an intimate experience of a flower. Spend some time observing a flower. Be open to discovering and cherishing the gift of your own wonder and delight.

Bloom where you are planted. It is always here and now.

13

CAREGIVING VS. CARETAKING
ANXIOUSLY HELPFUL OR ANXIOUSLY HELPLESS?

I completed an online personality type assessment at one time that outlined the various archetypes of our psyche/subconscious/underworld. I was anticipating some good news or affirmations about me and my lot in life.

Here are the results:

"You're the caregiver! Carl Jung identified this archetype in many goddesses and female role models throughout history. You're the mother figure: the selfless caregiver and helper. Everyone comes to you for advice. You truly love others as yourself and your greatest fear is selfishness and ingratitude. You manifest compassion and generosity. A Jungian psychologist would tell you to be careful not to be taken advantage of and never let yourself play the martyr."

It sounds noble or almost saintly. Right? Wrong! At least for me, it does not feel that way. I have spent almost a lifetime as a caregiver. At three years of age, I looked around my environment and had the thought, "Oh hell, I'm the oldest one here." Add to that, I am named for two of my old-maid great aunts, Martha and Lee, who were both caregivers of both sides of the family systems. That means that technically they never had a life of their own. They didn't marry or have relationships or children. They didn't have homes of their own. They lived with other family members and were most often the ones who were called when caregiving, nursing, midwifing, babysitting, recovery periods, and real hard work was needed. Further, add to it the curse from the Bible story of the "Martha, Martha, thou are busy with many things" aspect of things. (Luke 10:41) It is no wonder why a psychologist would caution me not to be a martyr.

Following are ten versions and translations of this particular Bible quote. Enough said!

New International Version
"Martha, Martha," the Lord answered, "you are worried and upset about many things."

New Living Translation
But the Lord said to her, "My dear Martha, you are worried and upset over all these details!"

English Standard Version
But the Lord answered her, "Martha, Martha, you are anxious and troubled about many things."

New American Standard Bible
But the Lord answered and said to her, "Martha, Martha, you are worried and bothered about so many things;"

King James Bible
And Jesus answered and said unto her, "Martha, Martha, thou art careful and troubled about many things."

Holman Christian Standard Bible
The Lord answered her, "Martha, Martha, you are worried and upset about many things."

International Standard Version
The Lord answered her, "Martha, Martha! You worry and fuss about a lot of things."

NET Bible
But the Lord answered her, "Martha, Martha, you are worried and troubled about many things."

Aramaic Bible in Plain English
But Yeshua answered and said to her, "Martha, Martha, you take pains and are troubled about many things."

Suffice it to say, I am still finding too many ways that anxiety drives me to seek, search, rescue, fix, advise, counsel, trouble, meddle, do what is not my responsibility, over-give physically/financially/emotionally/mentally, and spiritually, and in general, not mind my own business. The allure and temptation to martyr myself is quite dominant as well.

The good news is, I am more and more aware of it and therefore, it's easier to correct, undo, wake up, and choose another course for myself. When I fall off the wagon, I am more forgiving and understanding of myself, and I don't go as far off as before. There is progress. There is real hope. If there is hope for me, there is certainly hope for all.

Take the tests below and see what you can discover about you and your patterns or archetypes. See if you maybe are "anxiously needy" or "anxiously needing" to be needed. I'm sure somebody out there can relate to Saint Martha. Go easy on yourself!

Needy Caretakers	Needy Recipients
Need to be needed	Takers
Give endlessly	Quick to feel abandoned
The "take care of it all" person	Easily angered
Can't control their generosity	Not tolerant of disappointments
Volunteer for every job	Unable to forgive the mistakes of others
Do other's work	Too sensitive to being emotionally hurt
Please others at the expense of their own well-being	"Injustice collectors"

14

CRISIS

Webster defines crisis as:

1. A time of intense difficulty, trouble, or danger, "the current economic crisis"
2. Synonym: emergency, disaster, catastrophe, calamity; predicament, plight, mess, trouble, dire straits, difficulty, extremity, etc.
3. A time when a difficult or important decision must be made; "a crisis point of history"
4. Synonym; critical point, turning point, crossroads, watershed, head, moment of truth, zero hour, point of no return, doomsday. "The situation has reached crises."
5. The turning point of a disease when an important change takes place, indicating either recovery or death.

I have been reflecting lately on the way the word *crisis* strikes me when I hear it. A friend called and said she was heading out of town for a holiday weekend and received a crisis call before she got to the edge of town. After hearing her describe the situation, I could not relate to the request as a crisis. I heard another friend say her daughter was in a crisis and I asked what it meant. She replied, "Her life just doesn't work."

When I received the notice of the death of Robin Williams in September of 2014, I was as deeply affected by this news as I've ever been by the death of a celebrity. In fact, I was shocked at just how much I was affected by his death. I was filled with gratitude for his life and work and astonishingly awakened by the depth of the suffering of souls that have all the ways and means to get help and there is no way for them to help themselves, or for loved ones to help in many cases. That seems like a crisis to me.

What *is* crisis to me? In considering a response to this, like most, I first refer to some very personal experience with what I believed crisis to be. For me, crisis has meant; for example, a ruptured appendix, gangrene, peritonitis, coma at age fourteen. My baby brother died unexpectedly at the age of 40 from a massive heart attack. My dad had perforated bleeding ulcers and collapsed lungs routinely during his last couple years of life that required emergency transport and ICU care. I've had friends commit suicide and failed attempts of suicide. In each case, I thought the thing similar about the crisis was that it had a beginning and an end. I'm beginning to question whether it did or not. Death seems to mark the end, certainly of the physical. However, the crisis that causes the death, depression, despair, apathy, rage, disease, etc. does not seem to end. Where does that leave us?

I also think about the survivors of the crisis. Are they/we the ones who are stuck in crisis mode? What about when we can't help, when attempts fail or when the end means death? What about the survivors, the caregivers? When, or if, does it end for them?

What is your experience with crisis? Is it true crisis, or like me, is it a crisis when the plane doesn't take off on schedule, or when I receive a diagnosis I don't like? Or when the city floods and the basement leaks? Or when a loved one goes into rehab again? Or when my company fails and I'm unemployed? Or my partner has an affair? Or someone doesn't pay back the money I loaned in good faith? Or when the treatments are not working anymore? Or when someone simply doesn't want to suffer anymore?

These questions come to my mind and perhaps to yours. Yet, perhaps the most important question we want to ask is: Can we find peace in the mystery, the uncertainty, and the unanswered questions?

15

EMOTIONAL INTELLIGENCE

The five components of emotional intelligence, as defined by Daniel Goleman, are self-awareness, self-regulation, motivation, social skills, and empathy. We can be strong in some of these areas and weak in others, but we all have the power to improve any of them. Now, that is great news! Improvement is possible.

The following are some indicators that one is in the process of improving. I am committed to working on these throughout my lifetime.

How about you?

- You are curious.
- You are a great leader.
- You know your strengths and weaknesses.
- You know how to pay attention.
- When you are upset, you know why.
- You get along with most people.

- You care deeply about being a moral person.
- You take time to slow down and help others.
- After you fall, you get right back up.
- You are good at reading people's expressions.
- You are a good judge of character.
- You trust your gut.
- You've always been self-motivated.
- You know when to say no.

My primary focus has been to accept my own humanity and to accept the human phenomena. This includes anger, pain, suffering, and challenge that are all natural parts of human existence. In the past, I would more often think, "I shouldn't be this way," or "I should be over this now," or "how much work do I have to do to be free of this?" "Is this bad/wrong to be experiencing anything negative?"

When I took an online Emotional Quotient (EQ) test, I received a low score. Imagine my shock, especially after having taken several of these in the past and being so *proud* of my high scores. After having scored low on the empathy test earlier in the year, it really got me wondering about what progress is or is not possible. Here are the results of my test:

POOR EQ

People in this range often find themselves holding in emotions and feeling stress and anxiety. They seem to have less 'buffer' for dealing with pressure, change, difficult situations, and relationships. Some people also report depression or feeling 'lost' in life.

Are you allowing the 'winds' of change to direct you,

instead of setting your own course using an internal compass? Are you responding to life and its pressure with fear and insecurity rather than passion and purpose?

Studies of entrepreneurs, leaders, and employees at some of the world's top organizations reveal that EQ counts for twice as much as IQ and technical skills combined in defining who will be a star. Improving EQ results in better relationships, greater health, and a happier outlook on life!

AREAS TO WORK ON:

Given that self-awareness is the foundation of EQ, you might want to start here on the road to higher EQ.

Things to consider: What situations generally create pressure and stress for you? How are you handling these situations? What negative thoughts play over and over in your mind on a regular basis? Are these a true picture of reality? Are you afraid to share your needs and feelings with others? Is it because you are taking care of everyone else, being a martyr, or acting the strong, silent type? If we have trouble expressing our emotional needs, if we regularly put others' needs before our own, there's a good chance that we will one day wake up feeling empty, hostile, or depressed.

Don't let this happen to you! Take care of yourself! Express your key needs. It may be difficult at first, but research shows it will be a win-win. So move into the zone of discomfort to express those needs and you will be rewarded for your hard work several times over!

This is one of the key steps to building emotional intelligence. You'll be happier and those around you will understand you better. Be grateful for their feedback. Remember, if life is 10% what happens to us, and 90% how we respond, then we hold the power to create the lives we want.

What great questions to ask. My results were a wake-up call for me. What do we do when we feel anxious? How do we get intelligence quickly? What do we do in those moments? Counting to five, self-talk, taking dragon breaths (a kind of deep-breathing exercise) are simple and profoundly effective. For centuries, we've been directed and invited to do this.

Such strategies may seem simplistic, but researchers say they can have a profound effect. It is noted that repeatedly practicing these skills means they gradually become automatic. The ability to stop and calm down is foundational in those moments.

I am awake to and awakening to the reality of the power of the emotional field and how thinking shuts down when I'm reactive. With a few deep breaths and some practice at observing self, I am much more self-regulated. That new understanding telling me the truth about what is really running my show and moving in this new direction for my life seems like intelligence to me.

16

EVERYDAY MIRACLES

Have you considered the thought that you are a living, breathing miracle? Consider the gift that you are able to read a book. The fact that your mind is able to make sense of strings of letters on a page is absolutely miraculous —not to mention that your incredibly intuitive body woke itself up this morning giving you the gift of life on a new day.

If you don't believe in miracles, how about the fact that there are an estimated 7.3 billion humans inhabiting this earth all at the same time? Or, consider that the 7.3 billion of us are driving an estimated 1.3 billion cars on roads all around the world-mostly safely and sanely. Miracle? In addition, we drive 70 plus miles per hour and are kept in our lane by an invisible force, a painted white or yellow line on the road. How amazing is it that we have the innate ability to connect with anyone anywhere anytime with our heart? We have technology that literally allows us to connect, call, text,

Skype, video, record almost anything from anywhere anytime on our planet!

Take a look at your finger. Now consider for a moment that your fingerprint is 100% unique. There is no other fingerprint in the universe exactly the same as yours, even if you're an identical twin. Fingerprints are arranged in a pattern of spirals and loops. Fingerprint patterns are inherited but are never exactly identical.

Each of us is a miracle worker. Our ability to manage our daily schedule of work, rest, play, relationships, family, friends, homes, pets, traffic, weather, money, food, care for the physical body (ours and others), all in a matter of 24 hours is a "Wow" and then some! How amazing that we can experience emotions and feelings and not be bound by them, especially when we are in a jam—a traffic jam, a copier paper jam, a cancelled flight jam, a misunderstanding jam, a broken down vehicle jam, a bodily part jam—and the list goes on. We can simply move on, fix it, rearrange for it, adapt, reinvent, heal it, tow it, seek treatment and surrender to what cannot be changed.

It's a miracle that we can put any two or more of us together and call it a marriage, a relationship, a family, an employer, and not kill one another with our own unique and very different lenses on life, priorities, values, and default patterns of behavior. We are given many challenges and opportunities to grow, learn, develop and create thriving, loving, and miraculously dynamic relationships with others. Evolution is human learning from human sufferings.

In the thinking business I am in, offering questions and tools for us to observe and understand the basis for thoughts, I witness miraculous breakthroughs of clients and workshop attendees on a regular basis. These miracle workers report they find new ways of living their already miraculous lives with more joy, more gratitude, more peace, and more willingness to face what is simply what is. We can learn to at least be more objective and neutral when we find ourselves in a jam.

Our humanness is a miracle, for sure! I join with you on the journey exploring with wonder and appreciation the sunrises and sunsets, blooming flowers, births, space shuttles, ants finding their way into the kitchen cabinet, rivers that flow and oceans that roll.

17

FAITH

I feel a little cautious venturing into a topic as big as *faith*. While I believe that faith has carried me through every single frightening, painful, stressful, challenging experience of my life, I don't presume to know what it is or means.

How would you describe faith? With the changes in our world always in our face, now seems like a really good time to draw on the faith of our ancestors and our own integrity to move in the directions that create hope, faith and love in our own inner world.

I can look back on several experiences in my life and see the best and worst uses of faith in making my decisions and choices. One example of using faith is when I went to look for a job in areas for which I was not qualified. I applied for an Executive Assistant position at a bank and was told by the Human Resources Vice President that I was not qualified for the position. She invited me to go ahead and be interviewed for it however, as that would clear me for the protocols for another position for which I was qualified. Therefore I could skip some steps. I had faith that somehow I would get the job for which I wasn't qualified. I went into those interviews more confident, willing, and ready than I would have if I had not had that faith. Yes, I was offered the position I wanted.

On another occasion, I accepted a position in Fort Lauderdale, Florida. I had never lived more than an hour or so away from my home of Bugtussle, Kentucky. I had never been to Fort Lauderdale and I didn't know anyone there. Faith carried me along the way. I remember someone cautioning me about moving there and taking a "blind" offer on a job. I remember feeling this strange and deep peace about it and replied that the road back from Ft. Lauderdale was just as short as the road to it. Likely, that remark came out sarcastically, as that was my consciousness back then. However, I truly believed there was nothing to lose and plenty to experience.

On the other side of the spectrum, I offered my car keys to my alcoholic brother when I was leaving the country on a trip. I made a secret deal with God/Faith that "if there was a God," this decision would work out okay. Can you guess what happened? Yes, the car was totaled, my brother was not scratched and I had a transformation about what faith and sensibility is. I am now grossly aware that I humanly misunderstand most concepts and that reality is always in charge.

Faith is personal and mysterious. It is good (and

rewarding) to regularly take the time to review our own convictions and belief systems. They each carry consequences, implications, and infinite possibilities.

18

FEARLESSNESS

For as long as I can remember, my dad and mom both have told me that I was a good child, well behaved, didn't need to be told twice, and that I understood their directions before I was verbal. This left me curious as to what would be the cause of this type of response versus being a "hardhead," not behaving, having to be told over and over, not understanding, or disregarding parental direction. I suspect that fear was the underpinning for it—fear of disapproval, upsetting them, or being seen as bad.

Fear is such a painful, stressful existence even when we are not aware of it—the seeking for something, addicted to getting it, seeking also to avoid what is painful or stressful and emotionally traumatized when we don't get our way.

Imagine being free of seeking love, approval, appreciation, and acknowledgment. Imagine being free... period. Imagine.

My mother is deathly afraid of snakes, (according to her)

and according to the fact that she jumped out of a boat in a river one time because a small (according to my dad) snake fell into the boat from a tree. She caught her leg on the boat, tore the ligaments in the leg, and was on crutches for a week. When frightened, we regress into the smallest part of the brain, the reptilian brain, where we have a very limited repertoire of response—namely fight, flight or freeze.

I have an interesting relationship with rules. I value them and rebel against them too. The rules say, "Don't pick up a snake." I say, "Okay, I don't want to be snake bitten AND I don't want to live in fear of snakes." I've had several opportunities to look at this fear, including during a trip to Australia several years ago. While fearing the possibility of being bitten by a snake, I was actually open to transforming and transcending the fear too.

In addition to the fear of snakes, I am aware that others have a fear of heights. While this is not as much a fear for me, I can relate, particularly when I went hang gliding and had to step off a tall, tall cliff. I had to coax and seduce several friends to go on the high rides with me. There are rules there too: hands, feet, and heads, etc. stay in the ride please! This is not a rule I've been tempted to break so far.

I have a photo of me riding a roller coaster at Six Flags San Antonio. In the photo, it appears I am frightened. The truth is, I was terrified because a "precious, irreplaceable earring" that my friend Ardy (who was seated behind me) had insisted I wear this day, had just flown off my ear into the floor board of the roller coaster. I caught it under my foot and was very focused on keeping my foot solidly on it until the ride was over. Rule one: don't wear precious things that belong to other people. Actually, don't wear precious things regardless. It is much too stressful.

I love Independence Day! It is a reminder to me to let freedom ring and that I am no longer a hostage to fear. Step by step, we can liberate ourselves from any F.E.A.R.—False Evidence Appearing Real. What scary things are you willing to overcome, or to push the limits of?

I hold the FREEDOM possibility for me and for you—as REALITY. May we all discover the hero treasures inside ourselves.

19

_____

FIX | SELF

"Conjunction Junction.....What's Your Function?"
Remember that song? Are you singing it right now?
With my love for learning, it was one of my favorite shows.
It made for a fun way of learning that words had not only
meaning but also functions. I am a little less interested in
what our functions are and more concerned with our
functioning, no matter the function.

So how are you functioning? As a divine being in a
human experience, have you noticed you are sometimes
prone to patterns, upsets, confusion, edges, and bristling?

Recently, I used the comparison of being a funnel or a
sponge relative to our emotional functionality. When we are
in a situation in which we are facilitating a discussion or
processing a large amount of information, will we be more
effective as a funnel or a sponge? As a funnel, we can easily
and effectively process information and move the key points

to a desired end point, decision, or delivery. As a sponge, we may absorb or take on the information and be negatively impacted both physically and emotionally. This can leave us overwhelmed, over-saturated, or emotionally exhausted. The sponge, when it becomes full, cannot do its job. It's basically useless. While it took on the spill, it may end up far less effective. As oversaturated sponges, we may even leak, be soggy, and create little messes and cause more "clean up" work.

No matter what our function or current level of functioning, I believe at a core level we all desire to be our best selves. To be emotionally present and at the highest level of functionality, it is important that we learn to manage ourselves. This would require that we:

- Distinguish fact and feelings.
- Assume responsibility for our own feelings.
- Don't assume responsibility for other's feelings.
- Regulate our own anxiety.
- Define ourselves to others, stay in touch with them and where they are coming from.
- Do not insist or expect others to think, feel, or act as we do.
- Allow time for things to process—offer patience.
- Hang in there, persevere and be uncommonly motivated to see things through.
- Use a wide repertoire of responses, be resilient.
- Accept that anxiety, tension and pain are a part of the human learning process.

- Take a stand and maintain a more relaxed presence.
- Avoid thinking that sees others or situations as good/bad, black/white, wrong/right.

Can you imagine the difference in you if you were to integrate any one of these tenets? Now expand that further as you begin to show up in relationships differently with your spouse/partner/family/workplace/community/world with this type of clarity. Little baby steps go a long way in matters of emotional functioning.

I enjoy assessment tools that allow me to see patterned ways of being, that along with awareness, I have the opportunity to not only understand but also to change.

http://www.drcraigmalkin.com/the-narcissism-test is a link to a survey on our narcissism qualities. It's quick, easy, and quite powerful in its brilliant delivery of the full spectrum of narcissism. It clarifies that we are all narcissist. Therefore, we don't examine, am I a narcissist, but how am I narcissistic. Some narcissistic ways are healthy.

What is in your mind that you continue to avoid looking at? What's the price you pay for not looking, seeing and telling the truth about a situation? What's the payoff for keeping the focus on your pain, suffering, and misery? What are the consequences to your life for staying stuck in the old painful patterns you've adopted? What's another possibility for you? What is something that you are willing to do differently to create a different experience of what is?

It is important to remember the one thing in the world we can do something about—our own functioning and reaction to what is. Change what we can. Accept what we cannot and *know* the difference. When we know what to do, we do it. Follow our own internal guidance systems and stay the course. We can experience solid ground through our connection with our self and our SELF.

20

FOLLOWING OUR OWN GOALS

If you haven't experienced much anxiety lately, go spend a weekend with your family. Actually, it might not even take a full weekend. For some, all it takes is to talk to them on the phone, or have a meal or short visit. What's that about? All this anxiety when we get with our family of origin?

Research from Dr. Murray Bowen, a family therapy pioneer and Tennessee native, suggests that it is due to our self-differentiation process.

My experience is that being an authentic adult is hard work and a never-ending task. The pathway is routinely paved with difficulty and challenge. To become mature, spiritually and emotionally, every person faces the task of the differentiation of self.

Not to differentiate is to fuse (the failure to become a separate person) with others and to place responsibility on others (or on situations, predicaments, and hurdles) for the way in which our lives develop and for our feelings. To differentiate is to provide a platform for maximum growth and personal development for you and everyone in your circle of influence. A way to change the world is through one interaction and one relationship at a time.

I've had multiple opportunities to practice and apply this theory and I've experienced transformation when I am able to apply it as well.

One of the hardest practices has been to live by my own goals, not by others' expectations or goals for me.

I declared at three years of age that I would be a minister. This declaration received a wave of laughter from those family members listening and deepened the conviction in me to stay the course, even at such a young age. I didn't speak of it again for years, although the conviction was deeply held. I plotted, planned and adhered to a path to fulfill that calling at the age of 40.

I left home to pursue an education (the first in my family of origin to finish high school). Even against the family norm, I found non-traditional, creative ways to attend college. First, summer school, then CLEP, where you challenge the curriculum of a course, test yourself and receive full credit if you pass. I received the maximum amount of credit allowed for that option. I worked full time in multiple jobs, had employers who paid for tuition, went to night school and challenged systems to expand to support non-traditional ways of education. Over time, I received an AA Degree in Accounting, a BS degree in Organizational Management/Human Resources, a Masters of Religious Studies and a Doctorate in Divinity. My family did not attend any of the graduations of these various milestones, nor did I want or need them to do so. No conflict about it, simply an understanding that these were my things, not for them or about them.

My life work is to self-differentiate and the following are some practices I would like to share with you:

1. Define yourself to others and stay in touch with them (especially if they disagree).
2. Regulate your own anxiety (put the oxygen mask on you first).
3. Make a clear distinction between fact and feeling.
4. Profess your own values and beliefs without attacking or judging others.
5. Do not demand or expect that others should think, feel, or act as you do.
6. Accept differences between others and yourself.
7. Take responsibility for your own feelings, not accusing others as the cause.
8. Live by your own goals rather than by others' expectations of you.

So, as you move forward into a new life, a new way of being, resurrected from old patterned ways of being, emotional binds, multi-generational pressures and culture, may you realize the truth of who you are. May you move toward the graduation of your dreams, supported by me and the whole Universe. When it seems overwhelming, please "curb your dogma."

21

GRATEFUL | GR8FUL | GREAT-FULL

W hat if you woke up today with only the things you thanked God for yesterday? As you look at this, please, please skip the guilt and shame this question may bring — now, and for the rest of your life, for that matter.

I shared this question during a Sunday Service message and received comments from folks telling me how it woke them up, or how much they had benefited from using a gratitude journal and from the spiritual practice of gratitude.

As a child, I had a dream in which I was shown two giant keys, representing the keys to life. One of the keys was gratitude and the second key was forgiveness. This powerful direction for living has served as a guiding force all of my life and am I ever grateful for that guidance and awareness. I am not as coherent and integral in my life when I leave that clear path. Even though demonstrating gratitude requires energy and thought, I cannot think of a better use of either resource. Living from an attitude of gratitude is a goal – to maintain a conscious effort of being thankful.

I often receive thanks from clients and workshop participants for whatever it is they think I have done that has allowed for their learning, discovery, or awakening. I remind them to also thank and appreciate themselves—for all they have lived through, all they have accomplished, all they have given, all the ways they have served humanity and the world, and for all they have realized about God/Life.

Gratitude as self-expression can be found in random acts of kindness, through having compassion or tolerance, and one of my favorites—giving or doing something for someone anonymously. Demonstrate gratitude in your daily actions and watch life respond.

I encourage you to find at least five things each night for which you are grateful and write them in a journal or notebook. Do this for 30 days. Only list something once so that you don't repeat items. This exercise may be quick and easy, especially as you begin or when things are going great. It may require a little more looking and truth-seeking at times when things seem more difficult or stressful.

In the process of creating a gratitude journal, I have found that it becomes easier and a lot more joyful to recognize and appreciate what I have, rather than what I don't have. It does not matter so much what you put on the list since this is a personal discovery process. Your outlook and your actions are really what matters. Enjoy how your experience of life is impacted by this simple exercise. We receive blessings and we extend blessings to the world through our actions.

As you count your blessings in joy and enjoy your findings, then make generous choices for yourSelf and for those you love.

22

HAVE FUN | BE CRAZY | BE WEIRD

On the wall in my living space is a plaque that reads, "I am fairly certain that given a cape and a nice tiara, I could save the world." Now, I don't really believe there is anyone or anything to save anymore, but the cape and tiara are fun!

Since 1989, during my birthday month I have worn a birthday button the size of a dinner plate that reads, "It's my birthday, where's my present?" I don't just wear it on the actual birthday but for as many days before and after as possible.

Somewhere along the way, I also acquired a tiara or two, or three, to add to the celebratory ensemble. And, celebrate I have – with as much of the whole world as is willing to just let the smile, burst of laughter, stare, or squeal of delight just have its moment in them.

The fun has also been in people's reaction and non-reaction. They have appeared in sweet, subtle and generous gifts including smiles, wishes, hugs, bottles of champagne, cookies, backrubs, and the offer of a woman's husband of 47 years!! I found an honest "thank you and no" helpful along the way.

Imagine meeting a woman wearing a tiara and a bright, large button outwardly telling the world it's her birthday. What are your thoughts? Fun? Crazy? Obnoxious? Sweet? Fearless? Want one too? Remember, there are no new thoughts and none you are having that I haven't already had myself. Would a thought stop you from experiencing everything?

I have developed a deeper appreciation for the birthday button sentiment, "Where's my present?" The appreciation is for much more than sweet gifts and gestures. It is a valuable and meaningful question I ask myself: "Where's my presence?" Gratefully, I notice the more I am naturally present to myself, my presence for others also expands.

Now, that's a gift!

23

HEARTS CALLED TO SERVE

I am here to serve those who serve. That has been my calling since I was a child and I am grateful to have listened to that still small voice. Imagine my family's confusion and worry to hear their three-year-old firstborn telling them that she was going to be a minister—especially given that this was a period of time where they had not known of a woman minister, nor was it a calling with which they were familiar.

I can easily see where I get my servant's heart when I consider my momma's heart and how she has found very creative and extensive ways to serve. The topic of volunteering/serving came up during one of my visits home when I was driving my 77-year-old mother to volunteer at a local food pantry. I was not surprised that Momma would volunteer for this program even though she qualifies for its benefits. She has a servant's heart and she feels better when she is doing something for somebody.

So, there we were in the midst of what appeared to be hindrances – health challenges, having to drive in the rain, and seemingly needing more rest. Yet, we were joyfully headed to pass out boxes of food at 7:30 in the morning. Bringing a smile or joy to others is the heart of my momma's ministry.

We also make monthly visits to friends and relatives in the nursing home taking lunch, playing cards or just sharing community happenings. Momma is known for her homemade dishes and homegrown blooms of love that she generously and routinely shares with friends, neighbors, pharmacists and doctors' offices.

While we were en route to volunteer at the food pantry, there was a talk show on the radio stating volunteer statistics. The report stated that 25.3 percent of the population 16 years and older had volunteered for or through an organization during this last year. The main organization where volunteers worked was most often religious (33.3 percent of all volunteers). Many volunteers also worked at educational or youth-service organizations (25.1 percent) and social or community service organizations (14.4 percent).

These are the official reported volunteer hours. I can only imagine all the unregistered unofficial volunteer servant heart hours and missions that take place all over the world and right in our kitchens and neighborhoods that don't get officially recorded. Mother Teresa comes to mind as I think of servant-heartedness. Mother Teresa, who cared for the poor and outcast on the streets of Calcutta, is quoted, "I do nothing of my own. God does it. I am a pencil, a tiny bit of pencil with which God writes what he likes." God uses people to love and to care for our world. I aspire to live this out, in large and small ways. I like it.

How are you called to serve? Where are you being guided by the still, small voice?

What is your heart calling you to do? As you consider your many gifts, time, talent, energy and passion, take action and find the best and most meaningful way for you to serve. Whether or not you are officially volunteering, you may be surprised how often and where you are serving others.

Each and every time you tuck a child into bed, take a dog out for a walk, usher at church, check on a neighbor, take a coworker to lunch, donate money or walk for a cause, take a meal to a loved one, share a Facebook posting of a charitable event/opportunity, hold a hand, give a hug, return a call, answer a message, forgive, learn something new—you serve. These are rich, meaningful, precious ways to serve and to be served.

I don't claim to know or understand service. I do clearly understand the nature of divine humanity – be of some earthly good; leave the world a better place and there is no order to miracles, human touch and acts of kindness.

May you and I experience ever deepening ways to serve as we realize there is only ONE serving and only ONE to serve.

24

HOME IS WHERE THE HEART IS

I 've been at my mother's house more recently for a myriad of reasons, including I am in transition with where I will live, and to accompany her for medical care. I find it very easy to fly in and out of Nashville instead of the Louisville airport, and I am in a full swing of downsizing and organizing again. My family has enjoyed having me around more often and has actually requested me to stay with this new arrangement.

There is always a full schedule of activities even while I am in my Bugtussle home. These activities include making tomato juice and canning tomatoes. They also include weeding, weeding and more weeding, mulching, as well as cutting beautiful bouquets from the garden and sharing them with various boyfriends, doctors, pharmacists, and neighbors. I feel especially good about sharing the blooms with nursing-home residents. My favorite place for the flowers is for our great friend Grannie. She grew flowers for decades and shared them with Momma and the entire community.

Another heart space bonus of being home is our family pet, Spidey (official name Spider, named by Daddy before his death). I remember well the day we went to get Spidey. I had searched and researched extensively to find a mini dachshund, short hair, male, as that was the breed we had previously. He was a great match for the family, especially my dad. Spidey proved to be a real companion and a barrel of joy. I think we bonded that very first day. My nephew Wesley says that he knew I was his rescuer. Perhaps Wesley is right.

Daddy was in bed a lot the last few years he was alive and Spidey would hang out in the bed with him until Momma went to bed. Then, he would join Momma. They often teased about him going back and forth and referred to him as "Benedict Arnold." Spidey is very attached to me. He is like a shadow when I am home. He sits by me as close as he can and sleeps with me. This is not all that popular with Momma who believes he is "Benedict Arnolding" her when he does that.

One night, I let Spidey out for his business prior to bedtime. It was around 12:30 a.m. When he returned, he was very distressed. He couldn't put his right hind foot on the floor and he was yelping. I put him in the bed to see if he could rest and find some ease. I couldn't see anything visibly wrong with him. I had taken him into the vet's office that morning for nail clipping and there was no problem noted.

Spidey was distressed for many hours and just couldn't find any relief. He vomited and stayed lifeless in his bed until the next morning. I called the vet's office for an appointment and began to prepare to take him in. He was ten years old and had some other medical issues that made me wonder if it was his "time." I've asked Spidey several times, to be sure that it is crystal clear to me when it's time. I didn't have a sense that it was the end; however, I found myself preparing for it just in case. I asked Momma if she wanted to accompany us to the vet. She declined and I asked her if she was ready to say goodbye to Spidey. She cried and patted him in my arms, expressing her love for him and stating that she could not watch him suffer. I was not in panic, but I had mixed feelings of sadness about how serious it could be, and courage of wanting to be a really peaceful presence with Spidey during the process.

When I got to the vet's office, I was prepared to hear serious news and to have to make the decision. Instead, he saw immediately there was an infection in his right back foot, which the assistant had not detected that morning. He said his heart and lungs sounded great, recommended he lose some weight, gave him an antibiotic injection since he doesn't like pills at all, gave him a sedative/pain relief injection and believed he was going to be fine.

I asked him about providing a pain-relief formula to take home in preparation for another episode if needed. I had concerns about how Momma would handle Spidey should there be another occurrence. The vet was so kind, considerate, and assuring. He quickly informed me that he and/or his assistant would come to the house to treat and care for Spidey with just a phone call at any time of the day or night. He also assured me he would bring him into the clinic and care for him there for as long as needed, or euthanize him when it became necessary. He further stated he could actually euthanize him at home if that would support us when the time comes. While it is not something I want to think about, it was truly music to my ears to hear this level of care and possibilities for Spidey, Momma and me.

I'm happy to report Spidey made a full recovery in just 24 hours and was back in my shadow again. I'm also happy our vet is so willing to serve him and our family.

I am grateful for both our human and animal *hearts in connection,* and the ways the hearts find a home in each other.

25

IMAGINE

I magine not having your computer for one month.

Imagine not having access to any of your old emails.

Imagine not having any documents from your past.

Imagine paying for a backup system to prevent the above and it taking three consecutive weeks to restore the data files.

Imagine finding out it doesn't actually back up the application from your computer only the files, since you are on a Mac, not a PC.

Imagine having to locate the discs that contain your original software applications.

Imagine navigating all this from ten different cities, WiFi connectors and hotel rooms.

Imagine having to recreate all your user names and passwords for every site you utilize.

Imagine getting a new hard drive and logic board and

spending four weeks waiting for it to work right, and then finding out the RAM is defective too.

Imagine having to present for five straight days, four hours a day including livestream with a computer that is spinning at best.

Imagine how minutely small all this is when friends are having colon resections, open heart surgery, burying their 43-year-old mother, being terminated from jobs they love, receiving a cancer diagnosis, being shot during church services, and doubting if there is any good anywhere.

Imagine the temptation of the mind, the allure of the victimhood archetype, to focus and tantrum in reactivity to such inconveniences. Imagine the freedom to not have to focus on them. I recognize even in and through whatever is happening that I have the option, of free will to shift my focus to something more interesting, or meaningful, or integral to who and what I have come here to be. I am pretty sure on my deathbed that I won't be looking back on this day or this month and remembering a computer crash. I will be looking back and remembering a day and month where millions of Americans' health insurance was saved and the United States Constitution was amended in the direction of equality. Setbacks to some. Freedom to others. Reality.

Imagine the peace that is possible through any circumstances.

26

IN GIVING, WE RECEIVE
BE RADICAL

A re you ready to radically receive and give? Sow a little peace? Be the light of the world? Donate to something/someone? Feed the hungry? Radically, intentionally do loving acts? Find the *joy* of giving? Feel challenged by it?

WHAT IF:

- *You* are the light carrier the world is waiting for?
- *You* are the one who can bring it to life and others?
- *You* are the one to live it out?
- *You* are love, divinely loved and cannot do anything about it?

I accept this as truth. I am the one! At least, I am the one I can do something about. I am the one to send a donation to friends in the wake of a hurricane; to the various agencies quickly providing water in damaged areas; to organizations providing a gift to people who have been displaced.

In 2012, I facilitated a 24-hour "Birthday" celebration for humanity in Louisville, Kentucky. This Birth2012 event was held with the intention to join together 100 million people around the globe on that day.

Having been intimately involved with the Birth2012 project and A.C.E. (Agent of Conscious Evolution) I have an awareness that we are in the end stage of a pregnancy in which the world, which has been created and carried by our Mother-Father Creator, is ready to be reborn into the hands of conscious co-creators. This means we are evolving – re-creating.

I also had the opportunity in 2012 to share time with two of my super heroes of inspiration, the late Barbara Marx Hubbard and Marianne Williamson. I was participating in an A.C.E training and had the opportunity to connect with 3,000 global leaders who understand the time we are in. They are committed to be the *one* to create change.

Marianne and I share a dream to evolve our political system and she, too, is overly active in supporting charitable organizations that focus on a "hand-up" instead of a "hand-out." It doesn't take long in her or Barbara's presence, to know that neither one of these co-InSpiritors is waiting for life to happen. Barbara was 82, vocationally "aroused," and more active than ever. Talk about inspiring! They are each clearly aware they are a part of this larger universal life force and that *now* is the time to wake up and fulfill each of our callings. I am grateful for them and the myriad of other co-InSpiritors who have blessed and guided my path.

We are given so many opportunities to live with intention, fully awake to each other and to our broader/enlarged selves in the world. What opportunity will you radically seize to break through old ways of being and create anew?

If you haven't begun yet, it's not too late. Let's take a little journey together. Close your eyes and reach out your hand and heart to your loved ones. One by one, gather each of them into your heart space. Be sure to get those who have harmed you or who are estranged. We are being radical, remember? Connect with them. Now, extend that expanded warmth and love out to someone you don't know, that perhaps you meet at the bank, gas station or grocery store. Once you have connected with them, call to mind someone in another state or country that you know and connect your heart light with them. Hold them in your heart and surround each with your best blessing.

Now, extend this out across the globe. Literally hold in mind someone in another country and even an entire country—kids at play, workers in a field, all races, religions, social status, everyone. Wherever they are, hold them in your mind and heart with love. Do you see them? You are deeply connected with them. Offer this web of love from your highest consciousness. Bless each soul and their journey.

Receive as you have given. This creating is free, and one radical way to give to yourself, others and the world. Gift yourself and the world in thoughts and actions.

27

INNOCENTLY HUMAN

Have you had enough blame, shame and guilt to last a lifetime? When I ask this question of a group, it is not meant to be rhetorical. My intention is for each person who is able to hear the question, to actually answer it AND to get a sense of the power of the answer. While I most often receive an initial laugh when I pose the question, it is quickly followed by an "aha" moment of realizing there is another option. Shame, blame, and guilt can be observed sometimes instead of adding it to the reservoir of accumulation.

My answer to the above question is YES! I have had enough blame, shame, guilt, and all of their cousins, to last me the rest of my life. I have found that I don't get to pick when, where, and how much they arise.

Self-hate, martyrdom, less than, not enough, too much, and not good enough are just a few of the issues that I assuredly will get to experience and navigate through as long as I have a pulse.

How does it help anything—you, your family, your life, your workplace, your community—to live or operate any of these patterned false operating systems? Even though we know not to do these things, we still do. Until we truly embody and practice another way, they predictably will be subtly, or not so subtly, running the show.

My own experience of systematically, purposefully, and intentionally finding, piece-by-piece, the places where these types of thoughts have roots in my belief systems continues to allow me to live the kind of life that interests me, one that gives me the energy and stamina to fulfill my own mission and vision of serving those who serve.

In sessions with clients or group participants, a question I often ask to allow someone to open their eyes and heart to their own innocence is:

"What would you say to me or to your best friend if they were in your shoes, in a similar situation, having this experience, or going through what you are?"

It amazes me how wise, gentle, kind, and clear we are when offering support to others, and how we are often more unforgiving, harsher, and downright mean and unkind with ourselves.

How would you treat yourself if you looked back on your life objectively and all you have lived through and realized the true hero that you are of your own story?

I think we could all get down on our knees and bow down to our own true heroic selves with the ultimate love, appreciation and acknowledgment that we have so desperately been seeking from others.

As a facilitator of individuals and groups, I am time and again reminded of the miracle and resilience of our human spirit. I get to witness personal transformation as individuals do their work, questioning their thoughts and awaken to their belief systems that may no longer be serving them. In this, I am deeply humbled and reminded of our amazing capacity to shed skins, just like our snake friends—crawling out of some pretty deep holes, dark and stuck places.

I have witnessed lives literally transformed in every aspect—psychologically, emotionally, spiritually, physically, and financially. It is what inspires me to keep doing my own work and to keep offering tools, practices, offerings, invitations, and encouragement for others to see more options. Each time a truth is discovered and lived out in each of us, we are freed and I believe we are freeing it for generations to come.

So I'll do what I can and reach those I can. You do your part of self-realizing and self-awakening and together we can do what I can't do alone. We will all find our way back to innocence. Stay in the questioning; keep the mind/heart open to what is and what can be. Remember the Miracle Maker that you are as a co-creator of your own life experience. What a beautiful way to be re-born into our humanness, our innate Christ nature. Re-friend yourself. If you don't, then who will?

28

SELF-DIFFERENTIATION
WHAT? NO ONE TO BLAME?

I invite you to have a look at the table below.

Undifferentiated	Differentiated
Quickly offended, easily provoked, too sensitive	Self-managing, shapes environment, shows slow to recover, resourcefulness
Reactive, instinctive, automatic	Responsive, intentional, thoughtful
Underhanded, covert, flourishes in the dark	Open, light-shedding, aware
Demanding, willful, stubborn, resistant, unbending	Resilient, flexible, has a sense of proportion
Thinks in black/white or yes/no, intolerant of ambiguity, seeks final solution, wants all or nothing	Has breadth of understanding, allows time for things to process
Blames, criticizes, displaced, fault-finds, has poor discrimination	Takes responsibility for self, learns when challenged, defines self from within self
Uptight, serious, defensive	Relaxed, at ease, sensible
Competitive, either with or against, sees life as a contest, contemptuous	Takes turns, collaborates, stays in touch with others even when tension grows
Vague, non-specific, cloaked	Clear, objective, purposeful
Creates too little space and one-sided solutions	Creates space, options, and common goals

Now, imagine your life, relationships, and possibilities if you stopped doing the patterns on the left, began doing and increased doing the practices on the right.

Imagine even dropping just one of these steps, like blaming. How would that one thing change your life?

I have been doing deep spiritual inquiry and emotional process work throughout my entire life in some fashion or another: processes, education, intensives, programs and just down-right the hard way sometimes. I continue to be amazed at the emotional binds that have me blinded, blind-sided and powerfully in denial of the old patterns, cultural norms, and reactive ways to which I am subjected.

What unseen patterns are "killing" my relationships, peace of mind, growth, and life experiences?

Here is a sample of what I call my personal credo from the material and my favorite handout of all time—this speaks volumes since I have been through more workshops and degrees than anyone I know.

1. Define yourself to others and stay in touch with them.
2. Regulate your own anxiety.
3. Make a clear distinction between fact and feeling.
4. Profess your own values and beliefs without attacking or judging others.
5. Do not demand that others should think, feel, or act like you do.
6. Accept differences between others and yourself, knowing that differences alone will not cause differing.

7. Take responsibility for your own anger, frustration, or distress, not accusing others as the cause of your discomfort.

8. Live by your own goals rather than by others' expectations of you.

9. Refuse to coerce, will, or threaten others into taking responsibility for you (or your pain).

10. Refuse to be coerced, willed, threatened by others into taking responsibility for them (or their pain). (Source, Healthy Congregations Training Manual, www.healthycongregations.com)

While it seems simple to say "define yourself and stay in touch with others," I invite you to test it. Catch yourself in your patterns of distancing, conflict, silence, or cut-off when others disagree or challenge you. What would it be like to regulate your own anxiety and not have your peace hinge on the emotionality and mood of others?

Who would you be if you STOPPED being: quickly offended, easily provoked, sensitive, slow to recover, reactive, instinctive, underhanded, covert, demanding, willful, stubborn, resistant, unbending, intolerant of ambiguity, thinking black/white/yes/no/all/nothing, blaming, criticizing, displacing, fault-finding, uptight, serious, defensive, competitive, contemptuous, cloaked, vague, one-sided? Who would you be?

What would your life look like if you were: self-managing, regulated, resourceful, responsive, intentional, thoughtful, aware, open, resilient, flexible, understanding, allowing time for process, responsible for yourself.

What if you were a person who learned from challenges, relaxed, at ease, sensible, collaborate, clear, objective, purposeful, aware of options, goal oriented, GRATEFUL?

I invite you to discover the power of self-differentiation. I join you, with a heart full of gratitude, for all the pioneers and programs that have opened the way for me and the world.

29

THANKS GIVING | GIVING THANKS | THANKSGIVING

G ratitude is my favorite word in the world. It is, and has been, a spiritual practice of mine for most of my life. In fact, it has always seemed natural. It is not possible to not have something to be grateful for in every situation.

Gratitude emerged through the research of Brene` Brown, PhD., substantiating that gratitude is the antidote for the absence of joy. Every participant in the research who spoke of the ability to stay open to joy talked about the importance of practicing gratitude. Participants consistently described both joyfulness and gratitude as spiritual practices that were bound to a belief in human connectedness and a power greater than themselves.

I have studied and/or facilitated workshops using prosperity materials many times over the years and still find it fascinating and challenging to deepen my practice in the areas that are recommended in the arena of prosperity. For example:

Spiritual practice: Clear clutter.

Martha practice: Circulate energy, give things away, stretch myself.

I have had a practice of clearing for most of my life. I have given away households full of items, furniture, appliances, electronics, beds, jewelry, linens, clothes, shoes, etc. over the years. First, was my move to Nashville, Tennessee from Glasgow, Kentucky (suburb of Bugtussle) in 1989. I went from a big ranch house in the woods to a condo in the city. While circulating those possessions I had several awakenings. One was that I had kept all the nicer linens, dishes, etc. on hold and had not used them. The reality was I didn't even remember I had them until it was time to give them away. The good news is that folks got some really good items and the best news is I decided that day to use everything. The better it was, the more I used it. I stopped categorizing anything as the good stuff. Everything became the good stuff. Freedom!

The next wave of circulating/giving came when I moved from Nashville, Tennessee to Fort Lauderdale, Florida in 1994. This time from condo to condo; however, I moved into a furnished condo. Therefore, everything but big earrings, my luggage, and my convertible went to someone wonderful.

The next move was back from Ft. Lauderdale to Hendersonville, Tennessee (Nashville) in 1997. This time, instead of giving the things away, I put them into storage for a short time and then into a new condo. I had so much Tupperware and other essentials that they would not fit into the new place. A loud siren went off! Give-away is critically important. How could this accumulation happen, even when I was purposefully not accumulating?

Things went back into storage when I moved to Louisville, Kentucky in 1998. (All the moves, by the way, were for career advancement.) I was provided a corporate apartment by the company and didn't get the things out of storage for some time. When it came time to pay the storage bill for that year, it was $1600. Now, that was another awakening—paying that much money to store things I didn't want or need. So, wave number three of giving things away was straight from the storage bin to the lucky new owners. Lesson learned.

The last of the moves came when I moved from the apartment to "housesit" in other people's homes—Louisville, Kentucky in 2004. This was the most fun of all the waves of circulation. I removed the things I intended to keep and placed them in my new housesitting closet.

After moving what I was keeping, I opened the doors of the apartment and allowed friends, guests, strangers and congregants to come to the apartment and get what they wanted. This time, I accepted donations for some of the items, which strangely was much more uncomfortable than giving it all away. I got to directly witness people's fascination and shock at such an act. It ranged from people spending hours contemplating taking one single item to people with multiple gigantic lawn and leaf trash bags, filling them up and dragging them to their cars.

After everyone was gone for the night, I would open drawers, closets, boxes, etc. and refresh the apartment offerings for the next day's taking. My neighbor, Norm, said,

"This is a miracle. The more you give away, the more you have." He was so right. He still is.

On the final day of that wave of thanksgiving, I was relieved that it was over and very physically tired from a week of moving and packing and loading and people. I had asked a friend to bring her group from the Rescue Mission over to the house to get anything and everything that was left. I left the house open for them and arrived back home really tired, dreading having to clean the house to prepare the apartment for my exit. I discovered these amazing women had taken all that was left AND they had cleaned every inch of that apartment in the most exquisite of ways. They had cleaned the way that gratitude would clean. I understand the power of gratitude. They had to do that. They had to give what they had. I received it exponentially in every cell of my being.

I want to be clear about this. I don't think or believe it is spiritual to give your things away. If one is not careful, it becomes a new "identity"—the one who minimizes, or simplifies, or gives things away. However, I do believe giving is our nature and that giving and receiving are one transaction. I've realized and experienced this firsthand throughout the years and I am unspeakably grateful for it.

Other spiritual practices include:

Giving anonymously; to give without getting caught; to give without telling anyone; to give without anyone knowing you did it. Try it and see how it feels and try to outgive God. I dare you!

30

THE POWER OF A QUESTION

Have you ever considered the power of a question or realized the power of being able to respond with full integrity rather than to react? The symbol of the question mark seems to represent an invitation that loops into consideration and ends with a period, the place where the mind can come to rest. This rest may be an answer, a new discovery, a realization, the truth—the truth that sets us free. One thing I have learned is that reading about the truth or talking about the truth does not free me. What frees me is actually KNOWING the truth, a different polarity of mind.

I have enormous respect for what I consider the power of a question to the stuck, pattern-driven, scared mind. The questioning creates a pause in the current thoughts or thinking in consideration of a response—a new way of seeing. A different way of thinking and living it out results when thoughts, especially those that are stressful or frustrating, are met with a question, or the four questions, if you utilize Byron Katie's *The Work*.

The Work brilliantly provides an arena for the busy insanity of our minds to pause. Like trapeze artists flying through the air, or monkeys swinging from tree to tree, our thinking naturally swings from idea to idea, thought to thought, want to want, need to need, should to shouldn't, etc. In this, we find ourselves in patterns or belief systems that are no longer useful, helpful or supportive. Our B.S. (belief system) is the source of all suffering. Are you ready to shed your B.S.? Do you really want to know the truth, even if it means your thinking is off?

A question in and of itself is not asking anything of us, not even an answer. What would it look like to pause and actually entertain the thought being offered, to check in with yourself for an honest answer? Do you want to go to a movie? Will you marry me? Would you like butter on the popcorn? White or wheat bread? Sweet or unsweetened tea?

What about when you are questioning someone else? Notice the stress of the wanting, seeking something from them. What happens when you don't hear the answer you wanted or when you do not receive an answer or response at all? Who would you be, free of "wanting?" How would you be better off to actually consider every question for the sake of self-discovery?

I have benefited greatly by a practice of waiting for a question to be asked to me in communication with others. It has served me well at times when I am uncertain about the purpose of the communication taking place, or if communication is actually taking place with someone. Not to mention, it is just down-right easier to listen than to be swept up in the manipulation, controlling and posturing that is so stressful when I am trying to get my say in, be understood, righteous or a know-it-all. It is good to consider that the person speaking may just need a listener. Perhaps they are not expecting a response or answer, or certainly not advice or coaching. Have they even asked a question? From a still, clear and loving space, I can clarify this and meet them with understanding.

Where do you go with your questions? Google? Spiritual guides? Parents? Do you actually ask?

How about going inside? Have you asked *you*? Begin within. Wouldn't we all be just a little better off giving ourselves the freedom of asking and the gift of answering/receiving from our own wisdom?

What will you question today? What part of your B.S. are you willing to shed or breakthrough?

31

TRADITIONS

Traditions are inherited patterns of thought or action richly woven into the calendars of everyday living. Some of my family's traditions are pause points that I enjoy, as well as question deeply. I believe it is important to respect and uphold certain traditions and to also question and clarify whether or not these traditions are honest action for me.

A few years ago, I began a new tradition with my mom on Mother's Day. We spend the afternoon strolling through row after row of "Doyle's Iris Patch." This is a neighbor's heartfelt work in three full acres of irises that is an annual open house for our community.

I notice that I get to adjust my pace to accommodate Momma's new slower speed, therefore, really pausing, stopping and discussing the different colors and varieties, savoring the absolute splendor and beauty of each variety. It is, of course, hopeless to try to pick a favorite. These beautiful blooms, shapes, colors, nuances all represent humanity to me. I pray that as I continue to mature, I can see each person with as much awe and openness as I do these blooms.

I acquired my love for flowers from Momma. I remember being amazed at how "dog tired" she was from working long factory hours, yet she would still go out to garden every day. I now understand that it was therapy for her. I am not enlightened enough yet to love weeds or really tough nut grasses. I do appreciate what the weeding, tilling, sowing and tending reaps, especially as I cut flowers and prepare bouquets throughout the year to share with nursing home and hospitalized family and neighbors.

I treasure many of "Momma's Pearls"—her many wise and simple expressions—like "sweep under your own feet"—which means mind your own business. Now, that is a tradition I want to practice, live from, and pass along to generations to come.

Cooking and eating everything on the table is a family tradition that traces way back. Momma's memories include not having much to eat and not liking what they had. Even though she didn't like the gravy and biscuits left over from breakfast that she had to eat every day, she found resourceful ways to deal with it. She would trade the biscuits and gravy for a hot dog or bologna from another kid at school who didn't like their provisions either. This resilience, cooperation, and resourcefulness is one of my greatest genes. "FIND A WAY!" That's a tradition I want to pass down.

While I often cursed the patterns of eating too much, too often and only fried food for many years, I have some understanding of what the underpinning is and therefore can celebrate the love and life that was always present through that expression. I am left to take responsibility for changing the parts of it I can, being mindful of the patterns, accepting what I can't change and KNOWING the difference. That is truer for me.

One of my favorite family stories is of my momma playing softball—the first female to join the all-male softball team in junior high school. I believe my momma is a pioneer who would not let traditions stop her from breaking through gender roles in sports. She was willing to challenge the status quo, not necessarily because it was her dream, but because she had something to prove. She was naturally good at it too.

What have, or will, emotional family/relational binds cause you to do? Think of something you were told as a child that you believed just because a parent or a figure of authority said it – "You should clean your plate. Housework and dresses are for women. Yard work is for men. Women can't drive tow motors." What are some of your family belief systems and have you questioned the integrity of them for you as you find yourself participating in or passing them on to your next generations?

Rituals and traditions shape our families, creating a sense of unity, warmth and closeness. Traditions are the glue that keeps a family together as family members promote a sense of identity and a feeling of belonging. In his book, *The Intentional Family*, scholar William Doherty says that as family bonds are weakened by busy lifestyles, families can stay connected only by being intentional about maintaining important rituals and traditions.

Regular participation in meaningful traditions helps families overcome an inclination toward entropy or the tendency of a physical system to lose energy and coherence over time. The entropic family loses its sense of emotional closeness because members neglect the family's inner life and community ties. While I am committed to keeping our family ties, I am equally committed to not keeping the binds of the emotional ties – a life's work.

My family brings the Bugtussle and surrounding communities together in the fall for a barbecue because Daddy loved the community and realized how seldom we got together unless it was for a funeral. After he passed, we continued the tradition. It has become a community highlight as we barbecue pork shoulder and neighbors show up for hours sharing food, harvest, families, faith, stories, and lives.

Traditions don't have to be extravagant or require a lot of money or planning. Time-honored traditions can allow family members to have something to look forward to that provides them with a sense of assurance in our ever-changing world. That is no small thing.

32

TRANSFORMATION

I was struck recently listening to someone complain about mowing the grass. It was one of those comments that reached right into the heart, core, middle of my being. I paused to consider this feeling and what was awakening in me relative to it. I was remembering my dad's last few months alive and how he would say, "I wish I could mow the yard. I wish I could still work some, I wish that I..."

What is it that we are taking for granted? What would we wish for if we could no longer do or experience it? What has to be transformed in us to awaken us to the preciousness of what we have, what we are, and to stop taking anything for granted?

I'm sometimes weary of hearing the word transformation used in workshops, seminars, spiritual circles—and yes, I say it plenty too. I am also aware that without reflection and inquiry, it, like other concepts, is really meaningless.

When I use the word transformation, I mean that I have

a new way of seeing things. Perhaps, I have questioned a long held belief running through my mind and now see the pain of believing caused by the believing, not pain caused by someone or some situation. Others describe transformational experiences from doing work with me or through the deep inner work we do in programs and immersion processes. While I can relate, I can't actually know what they mean by it. I believe they mean their lives are easier; their relationships easier; that they experience more peace and less stress and feel more equipped to meet life on its terms. They report they can look at the past with less shame and guilt and are less frightened by the imagined future. I don't know of anything more gracious. What are the components of transformation for you? Are you willing to include NO COMPLAINING in your transformation?

What would it be like to look forward to grass-mowing, traffic jams, dirty looks, ingrown toenails, unwanted facial hairs, and yes, even death of our old way of being? Imagine understanding that we, like the caterpillar, have to become "goo" before we become the butterfly we are destined to be. If you understood and accepted this, what would frighten you?

The gigantic difference in my life has been my deepening understanding and realization that I don't have to like it *or* love it—turning to good, that is. And, I don't have to be at war with, afraid of, or hostage to, what is either.

Transformation of mind! Again.

33

WANTING: THE STRESS AND MISERY OF IT

I hear myself often saying that we are hard-wired for wanting and we were born wanting. Our first memory is of wanting something. Stop here for a minute and check for yourself. What is your very first memory? How old were you when you first began wanting attention, safety, approval, affection, value, to be noticed, cared for, fed, or understood?

Also, pause and consider the consequences throughout your life of what wanting has brought you! How do you react when you don't get what you want? I had a therapist once ask, "Martha, how long are you going to let your four-year-old self run your show?" I was so struck I couldn't even respond. Imagine the shock to my highly functioning, mature, self-realized, spiritual, responsible, wise self! Truth has a way of cutting into the roots of the matter. She was dead on, and I was the last to know. I've been researching the consequences of wanting and the basic internal life-force of wanting for a decade now. I've experienced first-hand the misery and seduction of wanting, and of getting, and not-getting. I've also been in the allure of thinking that enough wanting will make it happen, manifest it. I've thankfully realized that no amount of wanting can change what is. The integration of the wanting and not getting is mine to manage. I finally have a glimpse of what it means to hear: "The secret is wanting what you get, not getting what you want." I can't even want what I get sometimes, however, I can most often accept it is apparently what I need.

My internal tantrum can be mostly controlled. My outer expression can fake the misery inside pretty well. However, the inner world is the part that I'm working at shifting, accepting what I cannot change—changing what I can—and *knowing* the difference. I'm working on accepting that wanting is normal human phenomena, part of our humanity, part of my humanity. I've accepted that I can have wanting and wanting *not* have me.

Until a few years ago, I couldn't even hear wanting from others and simply listen. My over-responsible, seeking-to-be-a somebody, generous self heard all people's wants list as my "to do" list. It's a true affliction, or at least a gross misunderstanding. The more I can accept wanting in me and not make it wrong or problematic, the easier it is to understand it in others and compassionately respond instead of taking it on. Who would you be if you were free of wanting? How would your day look? How would you direct your energy to change what you can? Who would you be with less misery and stress?

May your misery lessen and lessen—ON PURPOSE!

34

WE ARE ALL DIAMONDS

"Sometimes we forget that deep inside we are all diamonds: pristine, flawless, and radiant. Instead, we identify with the layers of emotional baggage that cover our radiance. Have you been judging yourself lately and identifying with surface issues? Or have you been labeling others, undervaluing them, and not realizing that you are overlooking their essential beauty?"

Aren't these great questions? These words were shared on a card in a birthday scrapbook I once received as a gift. Life seems to always give me the perfect curriculum, map, presents and an eternal invitation to Presence.

How does one discover a diamond? It's doubtful we would just mosey on by and pick one up off the sidewalk, although anything is possible. We never know where we will find our true self.

More likely, an exploration and some work are necessary to discover something underneath the earth, hidden under surfaces, crusted over in layers, below anything an eye can see, invisible to our everyday vision, perhaps living in the underworld.

In our innocence and patterned conditioning, we are often hostage to fear of the dark or unknown. This is one of our greatest opportunities—to *not* be at war with the unknown, the underground, or the dark side of ourselves. When we choose to stay in the comfort of the known, the way we have always done something, or to let things be, we may never enjoy the fruit of what is awaiting us; the fruit that is momentarily beyond our reach, out of sight and out of safe traversing—out on the limb. Have you noticed that apples and oranges grow way out on the limb? It is up to us to "grow" out and get them.

With an adventurer's heart and spirit, it is possible to go mining to see what's under there, in our underworld. We are invited to go to the cave of the psyche, the soul, to be willing to excavate the nuggets of ourselves that are just waiting to be brought to the light. What precious soul diamonds have you discovered in your search?

A recent diamond discovery for me came from completing an exercise entitled "A Money Autobiography." My "knowing mind" tried to tell me there was nothing for me there since I had done this exercise several times in the past. Thankfully, my open and curious mind was willing to do it again. I remembered that the "knowing mind" has it backwards. When *it* says don't do it, that's not important; I turn those around and proceed by doing the opposite.

While looking at family-of-origin thoughts and patterns around money and then looking at where these are in me, I found a little thread of an old belief dangling. When I pulled it, it brought forth the story of a fear of being made fun of as a kid, which of course is still present in subtle and powerful ways. The willing, courageous explorer aspect in me allowed the images, feelings, and stories to come through me, to be expressed, to be understood. I could discover the gift of the thought and its falseness—snakes in the grass. My innocence was reclaimed. I could see me shining in there even through the fear, shame, guilt, and other muck.

I became a certified scuba diver a number of years ago, and of course, I had the opportunity to truly go down under, to experience fear *and* not be hostage to it. After having had training and guidance from an expert, the scuba diver prepares for an underwater adventure by taking a buddy, checking equipment functionality, donning a mask and oxygen tank, all with the anticipation of discoveries in a grandiose underworld. Exotically colored fish, beautiful coral, the sounds of whale calls, and even up close encounters with shark await. Are you willing to go "underwater," even if it requires moving through some fear and risktaking? What if your heart is waiting for you there?

Until you go within, you go without. Friends and clients often tell me that this thought has given them the courage to go beyond the surface and into the pitch-black darkness of their unchartered and unexplored territory. The self-realization process takes a dose of courage and a curiosity to take the next step, sometimes with no map or compass, but with a lot of help and kisses from our underworld friends.

My journey to unfold self, penetrate the patterns, and self-realize has included a myriad of practices. One of these is meditation as a tool to observe the mind. Even in this arena, there is a wide range of experiences possible. I share these with you as resources and in gratitude for the ways in which they serve me, not to tell you how to do it.

Transcendental Meditation (http://www.tm.org) was an easy and natural practice for me that required I sit quietly for 30-minute sessions, repeating a mantra I received from the teacher to keep my mind focused.

The Work, Loving What Is (http://www.thework.com) is a series of really simple questions used to penetrate the closed, stuck, fearful mind to get to the truth of reality. We discover that we have everything backwards. Reality is kinder than the thinking.

Vipassana Meditation (http://www.dhamma.org) is simply observing sensations, no mantra, no visions, no distractions. Instead, it is a direct experience of sensation—the nature of which is always changing—practicing only observing, no reaction and with clear certainty that 100% of everything is rising and passing. Everything is always changing, impermanent, whether it is the deepest joy or the deepest despair. Painful, violent, scary or disturbing sensations or images may emerge or rise and through observing them; you can see that they come and go. Practicing Vipassana is to remain equanimous regardless of what thought or sensation is arising.

It is time to penetrate the lies, myths, fantasies of the mind and look to the real truth of what's inside. Know the truth—that you are unique, fabulous, brilliant, and priceless. This essence shines in all of us. We are all diamonds and we can't do anything about it.

35

WHAT IS A SABBATICAL?

The term "sabbatical" actually was derived from the biblical Sabbath which serves an ancient human need to build periods of rest and rejuvenation into a lifetime. Anyone can take a sabbatical. A sabbatical is simply getting an extended leave from normal daily activities or work to pursue a break.

People traditionally take a sabbatical to fulfill a goal. The key is to get away, renew, refresh, revitalize, rejuvenate, re-create, and remember what is important.

My sabbaticals are a time to unplug, get quieter, sit still inside, and explore the world outside. For my first sabbatical, I went on a dream cruise to the French Polynesian islands, including Bora Bora, Moorea, Tahiti, New Zealand, and Australia. It was unspeakably wonderful and met all the goals and desires I had to refresh and renew.

While I had been threatening to take a world cruise that

would last three to six months, I opted for the 30 days instead. I discovered that 30 days was the perfect formula for me. It's really good to know and I'm really glad I tested it out instead of following my knee jerk, "I'm getting exhausted and must survive" thinking.

When my sabbatical concluded, I immediately planned another 30-day sabbatical for the following two years. The first year began with a big life transition out of the living quarters I'd been blessed to be in for nine years. I didn't know where "my room" was going to be and I didn't mind the period of wilderness and uncertainty. As I had given away most of my possessions and moved into wilderness at least four times over the last couple of decades, I had become accustomed to uncertainty. It felt like it was an important part of my journey to continue to detach from things, places, ways and belongings, as well as explore what the next iteration of life held for me.

I value the time of sabbatical and the benefits are clear. It also seems like integrity for me. I am wisely committed to not only setting aside purposeful, meaningful, intentional time for this, but to find day-to-day and moment-to-moment ways to renew and restore as well. I have witnessed teachers, leaders, friends, and yes even my mother, build in breaks from the normal routines and pressures of professions, family, relationships, health and beyond.

I invite you to keep sacred your times of renewal, restoration and resilience. Let's begin right now with a deep full breath or three. And, with your next hot cup of tea or coffee, soak in the life of it. Pull out that calendar and put something fun in there, something to look forward to.

Unplug that computer or phone and let the battery run down, then use the time they are recharging to do the same for your soul. You know to do it. You know the consequences of not doing it. Choose again; and choose wisely.

36

WHAT WORKS, WORKS

I travel about ninety percent of the time. I'm astounded at how much activity there is in my life and frankly how much stillness within the activity. My gratitude for this phenomenon is unspeakable.

I get to witness the most enlightened parts of humanity throughout airports, taxis, hotels, restaurant servers, rental-car facilities, sky caps, porters, shuttle-bus drivers, retreat-center staffs, and through my most endearing familial and friends' relationships.

I receive feedback that I am lucky, and I have the same thought. I also have the diligent and concrete practices for more than 50 years now that keep me in this direction.

Forgiveness has been a giant key for my life. I've written about it many times and the power of that daily, and literally, moment-to-moment practice. I seldom experience any more deep affronts of any kind. I have realized that the more subtle the offense or the feeling effect of the offense, the deeper and more powerful the liberation. I can see it is concepts and the meaning I give them that cause this pain and suffering. Therefore, I can let go of the meaning I've assigned to it, turn it around to accepting human beings doing what human beings do, and loosen it immediately. I don't have to like it. I sure don't have to love it or condone it. Forgiveness doesn't make it right or okay. It just is.

Gratitude is my second giant key of practices. Even when the toast is burnt, I can be grateful for the bread, the toaster, what else is available to eat, the bounty, and the broader spectrum of "in the big scheme of things." This is *not* a big deal. I've practiced gratitude via speaking it, sending gratitude letters and notes (even to those I believed hurt me), counting blessings, gratitude lists, gratitude journals and training/re-directing my mind in this powerful direction.

OTHER ENDURING PRACTICES INCLUDE:

ACCOMPANY AND CONVENE:

To visit with people, be available, present in others' lives and my own, to share gifts and talents, to visit, care, listen, and encourage.

We did this as a family growing up. We called it "let's go see so and so." Go see. Be seen. I do this now by visiting a nursing home once a month to bless folks there. I take flowers, and gifts; give hugs, pats, and smiles as I pass through. I also do this by keeping important relationships scheduled in my calendar for time away together, visits, trips, vacations together and spending time with them when I'm near their cities.

CONNECT:

To create relationship systems, to know and be known, to ask others for insight, support, ideas, experience and share with them.

I do this through Facebook, Twitter, newsletters, recording my talks, posting the videos, calling while I drive, emailing, sending approximately 150 birthday cards a year, and continuing to find innovative ways to connect.

GIVE SANCTUARY:

To provide and maintain a safe place, to allow room to breathe, to allow space for rest, recovery, time for process.

I do this by holding silence when I visit people, taking time to rest together on the porch or couch. I also facilitate four retreats a year that provide a space for renewal for others and me.

BLESS:

To make things special, to bestow well-wishes, celebrate milestones, positive vibe energy, and hold perfect thoughts for people.

Whether in person, through the mail, postings, cards, prayers or simply through heart energy, I confer blessings to be seen and unseen.

PRAYER:

Daily and systematic prayer.

When I can't sleep, I start with A and go to Z and pray for every person I know whose name begins with that letter. I also call the 24-hour prayer line for Silent Unity and have prayers spoken and letters of support sent to folks. This returns me to connecting, convening, giving sanctuary, and blessing. I repeat. What works, works.

37

WHO WOULD YOU BE WITHOUT YOUR STORY?

F REE is the response I most often hear from participants and clients when I ask, "Who would you be without your story?" Your turn. Stop reading and just experience the word FREE in your body and soul. Can you feel that? Who would you be as freedom?

The Work (www.thework.com) is about discovering where we are hostage to our thinking and then realizing that believing our thoughts is the only thing keeping us from freedom. If we don't question our thoughts, we are stuck reacting to a past that's over and an imagined future that doesn't exist. With the questioning of our mind, we develop an understanding that freedom is something only we can give ourselves. No one else can do it for us, give it to us, or take it away from us.

The good news is: we are responsible for our own freedom. The bad news is: we are responsible for our own freedom.

I received a breast-cancer diagnosis from a routine mammogram. When the doctor called with the results of the biopsy, she struggled to communicate the "bad news." I was open to the results ("free," so to speak) and therefore, was able to minister to the doctor, and myself, in a meaningful way. As odd as it sounds, I did not mind having the cancer. I didn't assign it any meaning and was open to following the doctor's advice and directions. To this day, I haven't been disturbed or stressed about having cancer. The mind naturally wants to call cancer/disease *bad*, and health *good*. I just didn't experience it that way. So far, it has not affected me in any way other than good. Throughout the process of surgeries and recovery visits, I continued ministering to doctors, nurses, friends and my family (who did have fear about cancer).

If I have thoughts about a future with cancer, I have no freedom. I am in an imagined future and must return to reality, which is stress-free and kinder.

As I continue to do my work, I become practiced in immediately questioning concepts such as cancer, my breast, my body, and even death. Even though I was hearing *my* breast, I didn't believe it was *my* breast. I also questioned what the worst thing that could happen was and experienced grace in finding that nothing frightening came in response. While some would be concerned about losing a breast or even their life, that wasn't my reality. Is this the truth or denial? It's been over 13 years now. Time will tell.

Where did we get the idea that illness, cancer, and disease weren't going to be a part of this human experience? For now, reality reports something different, and I am open to a reality where it does not exist. I am "dis-eased" when I oppose reality and when I am hostage to fear. What are you hostage to?

Who would you be without fear? Daddy would say, "People are not really living because they are too afraid of dying." Is this true for you? No-body makes it out of here alive. Have you noticed? We die right on time, so perhaps we can relax a bit, live a little, and find some grace and gratitude for what we do have and can do.

I believe life brings us exactly what we need to call forth our next greatest version of ourselves. We are here to self-realize, and that includes challenges. Yet, peace is an option even in the challenges.

On the day of my mastectomy/reconstruction surgery, I wore a pair of giant heart glasses and a button that said, "Stop Staring at My Breasts." That really brought a new perspective to surgery day. As doctors and nurses paraded in to prepare me for surgery, with their to-do lists and "serious questions and tasks," imagine their surprise as my first task for them was to have their picture taken with me wearing the big pink heart glasses. Staff from lab, anesthesia, organ donation, clinical trials, and other areas of the hospital came to check out the party in my pre-op room. They sang Christmas carols, wore the glasses, took pictures, and laughed. The last thing I heard as I headed to surgery was laughter. The first thing I heard upon awakening from surgery was, "Ms. Creek, here's your button back" with laughter and gratitude. The spirit of "all is well" was, and is, alive when we are free to experience life exactly as it is. We can bring ease to disease.

After eight hours of surgery, the doctor came into my room to check on me. I got out of bed, still attached to drains, tubes and machines. He was concerned, thinking that I was not coherent after anesthesia and encouraged me to get back in bed so as not to hurt myself. Actually, I was just naturally greeting him with a hug. He was shocked as he had never seen a mastectomy patient out of the bed that quickly with complete range of motion in the arm and body and who was ready to go home. The operating team was discussing my case with the unbelievable outcomes and they surmised that my spirit was a large part of it. Cancer didn't affect my spirit. I am grateful for that.

I also define freedom as being open and willing to do it all wrong, without trying to do it right. It's easier and a heck of a lot more fun! A closed, afraid, stuck mind has no options. I have the option to free myself over and over as life brings what it brings.

There are two ways to experience cancer—in fear or in peace. There are two ways to experience life—in fear or in peace. I've been cancer-free for 13 years and it taught me a great deal about life.

38

WISDOM AND INTUITION WITH A GPS
GOD'S POSITIONING SYSTEM

During my dad's sickness and death process, I often believed he was intensely and horribly suffering. In the physical realm there was plenty evidence to substantiate this.

On one memorable occasion, I noticed blood coming from his gastric feeding tube. I immediately called 911. He was admitted to the ICU for a ruptured bleeding ulcer (unrelated to the progressive cancer). He eventually needed 17 pints of blood and plasma before surgery repaired the ulcer. He remained in critical condition for several days and was not expected to live. We have a family edict, legal directives, and commitment to forego any life support for the purposes of prolonging life. During every 12-hour shift, the nurses would approach me in the waiting area of the ICU and notify me of his critical condition, inform me that he is likely to die and that, with a DNR (Do Not Resuscitate) order in place, they could not save him. I assured them each time that I understood clearly and was carrying out his wishes. I felt at peace and empowered by the clarity of what I believed was mine to do.

During that ICU period, he developed a sudden lung problem that required him to go on a ventilator or die. Although his strong wishes were not to be put on a ventilator and I had agreed legally to execute those wishes, I went inside my own heart's wisdom and asked what to do. I followed what I call intuition; guidance or an unspeakable knowing—a GPS (God's Positioning System)—that transcends the physical and emotional aspects of being. I agreed for him to be put on the ventilator.

He had been unconscious and in what is referred to as ICU psychosis (disoriented, grimacing, groaning, etc.) for more than a week and in critical condition. During this time, he had no obvious awareness of time, place or people. It was the most intense and unbearable suffering I had ever witnessed. When they started to insert the ventilator, I was in the room and holding his hand. For the first time in weeks, he opened his eyes, looked directly into my eyes, squeezed my hand so tightly that his nails left imprints in my hand, and clearly said to me, "STOP THIS." I was as calm as I had ever been and again simply went into my heart for guidance.

My intuition was to proceed even though my agreement and the well-laid-out care plan was to *not* do this very thing. I want to live without regret. I knew that not following my strong intuitive wisdom would be an abandonment of my *Self* and my dad. I was willing to be accountable for my actions. My dad came off the ventilator the next day and began to improve. He eventually recovered from the ulcer and complicated blood loss completely. I don't believe I will ever understand the seen and unseen miracles of our life's journey.

On our way home from the hospital, I apologized to my dad for ignoring his wishes about ventilators and life support. I asked him how I could make it right with him and offered to be removed as his medical directive executor.

Surprisingly, he did not remember anything after we left the house weeks before. He had no recall or awareness of being on a ventilator. He had no memory of telling me to stop it. He had no recall or experience of any suffering. No suffering at all!

He was suffering! Is that true? *The Work* (www. thework.com) has taught me to question everything. When I question what is, I am not in false beliefs and a made-up story about what is occurring. Clarity, strength, and wisdom that are seldom accessed can be reached and will emerge to show new possibilities.

My belief that he was suffering created suffering, especially in me, as I projected it. What a relief to know that the appearance of suffering is not always suffering. When I believe they are suffering, I suffer. That exponentially increases it. When they are actually suffering, if I join their pain again, I have exponentially increased it. Wisdom reminds me to stay free of suffering when I can. That leaves at least one of us here to serve those who need it.

I do not recommend people forgo agreements or disregard commitments. I know however, that the process of humanity is not black and white and the wisdom and intuition that guides all possibility is always available to me when I dare to listen or be still and know.

I am still learning. Suffering is, and has been, a great teacher. Anxiety, pain, and suffering are part of the human condition. In all things, and especially in suffering, God is there. I cherish that belief. I am grateful for experience.

Wisdom comes from the heart. The intellect is important too, for it offers information, but true wisdom comes from the heart. It is in the heart that information, emotion and truth swirl together and combine to create true wisdom. Let the mind provide information when needed, but always follow your internal intuitive GPS.

YOUR MAP

Dear friends; I invite you to use Martha's Pearls as a map to love and self-realization. I pray these words are practically applied for your own liberation and joy. These words were written to nurture and bless your spiritual journey of life. Look down the road and dream about how amazing a world of Love can be as you journey Home! So be it! Go to www.marthacreek.com to contact me and learn more.

ABOUT THE AUTHOR

Martha Creek is a self-employed ministry consultant, speaker, coach, minister, leader and workshop facilitator. She has served in a ministerial role in both Religious Science and Unity Churches. Her extensive background and specialized training – Seminary, Hoffman Institute, Byron Katie International School, Healthy Congregations and Family Systems, Lombard Mennonite Peace Center, and more – support her in being able to deliver a great deal of information in a profoundly simple, dynamic and attainable way.

Being a master of the art of right questioning, Martha is able to call forth the most stubborn, self-defeating and embedded patterns in a person while inviting people into a new reality.

Martha's mission and vision is concise and clear: "Go within or go without."

For more information about Martha Creek, her work, schedule of events and the resources she has to offer, visit her website at www.marthacreek.com.